COME IN NUMBER 37
ROB LEE

Carl Liddle, who collaborated with Rob Lee in writing this book, is currently Northern Football Correspondent for the *Express* and *Sunday Express*. He began his career in sports journalism in 1988 with the *Shields Gazette*, covering football and, in particular, Sunderland AFC. From 1992–97 he reported on Newcastle FC for the Sunderland Echo Group, before joining the Press Association for one year. He is a regular feature writer for *Match* and *Shoot* magazines.

COME IN NUMBER 37
ROB LEE

the autobiography

ROB LEE with CARL LIDDLE

CollinsWillow

An Imprint of HarperCollinsPublishers

First published in hardback in 2000
by CollinsWillow
an imprint of HarperCollins*Publishers* London

First published in paperback in 2001

The HarperCollins website address is: www.**fireandwater**.com

© Rob Lee 2000, 2001

1 3 5 7 9 8 6 4 2

A CIP catalogue record for this book is
available from the British Library

ISBN 0-00-710289-5

Typeset by Mick Sanders

Printed and bound in Great Britain by
Clays Ltd, St Ives plc

Photographic acknowledgements
All photographs supplied by the author with the exception of
the following: **Allsport** p 12 (top left); **Coloursport** p 14 (all);
Empics p 10 (bottom left), p 11 (bottom), p 12 (bottom);
Tom Morris p 2 (bottom right), p 3 (centre and bottom), p 4 (all);
Newcastle Chronicle and Journal p 6 (top left);
Newcastle United FC p 6 (top and bottom), p 8 (centre),
p 9, p 10 (bottom right), p 15 (top); **Popperfoto** p 5

Career statistics provided courtesy of
Colin Cameron (Charlton) and Mark Jensen (Newcastle)

CONTENTS

ACKNOWLEDGEMENTS

I would like to thank my agent John Morris and co-author Carl Liddle for their help and support during the writing of this book; thanks to mum, dad, Mark and Dean for their encouragement over the years. But most of all I would like to dedicate this book to my wife Anna, our two boys, Oliver and Elliot, and our little daughter Megan.

CHAPTER ONE

NEVER A DULL MOMENT

When the number 37 was flashed up as Bobby Robson withdrew me ten minutes from the end of Newcastle's final game of the 1999/2000 season, he signalled the end of nine of the most mixed up, frustrating, and at times bewildering months of my whole career.

A game that I have loved and has given me so much enjoyment had accepted me back into the fold, but even I had doubted earlier in the season whether I'd ever wear the cherished black and white of Newcastle United again.

Let me state I believe strongly in fate and the hand it deals out to us all. Generally I have been dealt a good hand, throughout my career the good times having far outweighed the bad. But as I look back on schoolboy years growing up in Hornchurch, if someone had told me almost three decades ago – when the very sight of a professional footballer and his sponsored car left me daydreaming of following in his footsteps – that I would become the centre of controversy when Ruud Gullit, one of Holland's greatest ever players, felt so little of me that he didn't even give me a squad number for the start of the 1999/2000 season, then quite frankly I wouldn't have believed it!

It is truly remarkable how you mature to take almost anything in your stride – if you retain your self belief. Many would describe me now as being a quite stubborn character but in this multi-million-pound business I believe stubbornness is not such a bad thing.

The late, great Frank Sinatra often sang, 'Regrets I have a few … too few to mention', how those words aptly sum up my career in football. I have been loyal to my only two professional clubs, Charlton Athletic and latterly Newcastle United, and in return they have supported me one hundred per cent – but for one man.

Failing to figure in any of Gullit's plans during the later stages of his troubled tenure in charge of Newcastle, it would have been easy to quit and throw in the towel. However, at no stage was I prepared to bottle it. That would have meant accepting I was no longer wanted by a club with which I had developed, over an eight-season stay, a very strong emotional bond.

Maybe if over my playing career I am to be judged solely on how many things I have won, then I have not always fulfilled my dreams. But for me it is so important to enjoy myself and for the most part I have done so. I have been so lucky and I know it.

So much has happened to me during the last year, the end of eight years in the crazy up and down rollercoaster existence which is Newcastle United Football Club. It has prompted me to sit down and pen the autobiography of my playing career. I still hope to continue in the game once I hang up my boots but hopefully that is a tale for another time.

But whatever has happened during my time on Tyneside, one thing is certain: I remain proud after the people I care about most, our wonderful fans, handed me the tag of 'Honorary Geordie.'

The reception I received from them as I left the field on the final day of the 1999/2000 season meant the world to me. I was substituted ten minutes from the end of the match in which we were beating an under-strength Arsenal side, preparing as they were for the UEFA Cup final against Galatasaray. They gave me a tremendous ovation as I neared our dug-out.

It has often been said that the Geordie fans are the most passionate supporters in England, or even the world. Of that I'm in no doubt. It's because they're true supporters of the game of football, not just their own side. You can take, as an example, that game against Arsenal. Our fans gave their Nigerian international Kanu a wonderful reception as he left the field minutes before I was subbed.

Throughout the many years of mediocrity, with the occasional sunny interlude, they have stuck by their club. Now, as I enter the twilight years of my career, I feel it is one of my great unfinished goals, if humanly possible, to reward the fans by winning a major trophy for them. As the fans are only too willing to tell me: 'There will be no party to match the one the whole of Tyneside will have when we win something major, factories will shut down for days.'

Unless you live amongst them, no-one knows just how much our supporters will party. No-one knows just what a trophy for Newcastle United really means to them, unless you stick around and become one of them. I sincerely hope they feel I have earned that right.

Those much appreciated ovations, allied to regular chants of 'Robert Lee, Robert Lee, Robert Lee', which come booming out from all four sides of the ever expanding St James' Park, mean so much. It is those moments you play for.

Without any doubt, the fans' backing helped me stay firm. Their support during the lowest point of my career, when I was ostracised by Gullit and not even given a squad number for the start of the 1999/2000 season, helped me remain steadfast and determined to win my personal fight to win back my place back in the side. Even when many friends had begun to question my sanity in sticking it out, I dug deep. They all asked me the same question – why did I want to stay at the club when it was then managed by someone who didn't intend to include me in any of his plans?

There were plenty of clubs, I was told, willing to rescue and then kickstart my career but maybe I am too stubborn. By this stage in my time at Newcastle I had already seen the rise and fall of two men I think very highly of, Kevin Keegan and Kenny Dalglish, and I was determined not to follow them out of Tyneside.

All along I believed fate would be good to me, that it would continue to deal me a good hand and that I would still be with the Magpies long after the then manager had flown his Tyneside nest, and so it eventually proved. As the curtain finally fell on a traumatic season, one which had began so disastrously for anyone with the club's immediate future at heart, it left me feeling fully vindicated in remaining so stubborn.

Fortunately for me and Newcastle, Gullit left,

Bobby Robson arrived and the gloom was immediately lifted. In fact my only disappointment during the uplifting, and at times stirring, months under Mr Robson, was to score my first and only goal of the season in the FA Cup semi-final in early April at Wembley, of all places, and then have to once again endure the gut- wrenching walk down the tunnel after finishing up on the losing side.

Still, things were much better than the pain and frustration as the season started. It is fair to say that during late August 1999, not only was I expecting to be on my bike but Alan Shearer felt the same. We both felt alienated and the team wasn't getting results on the pitch. We were rock bottom of the league by 14 August and there appeared no end in sight. In my opinion, during those disastrous weeks Newcastle United was eventually only a few minutes – one victory – away from long-term downfall, even disaster. The club was heading in only one direction, back to the first division. The Dutchman seemed so close to forcing his managerial decisions upon the club's Board of Directors, that it looked as if he would leave myself and Alan with no alternative but to go. In the end it was only the club's continued run of bad results which spelt the end for him.

Everything lay in the balance for me and my family. How differently things could have turned out if it had not been for those late August results. I might never have been given back a shirt and squad number, certainly not the way things were heading under Gullit.

More catastrophically for a club with such proud traditions as Newcastle, their number nine would not have been around on Tyneside to ever again prove to critics, not himself – he has never doubted his own ability – that given service, and enough of it, he will always score goals.

It really was that close to completely falling apart, in my opinion, as I became increasingly aware that Gullit could not put things right. Then came the crunch game. I felt at the time it was so important, not just thinking selfishly, but for the club as a whole, that the team Gullit selected for the derby clash with Sunderland on 25 August 1999 should lose – knowing just what that might mean in the greater scheme of things.

The feeling of relief was tangible when it was announced, within hours of the 2–1 defeat by Peter Reid's men, that Gullit had left the club. He arrived at St James' for the last time to make official his departure, delivering a carefully worded, hardly emotive, speech to the local and national media. That relief was felt by many, many more people than just Alan and me.

Even as the club's supporters were shaking hands with Gullit and wishing him luck in the future, rumours about who would be next were already circulating around Tyneside, a great bastion of speculation such is the fans' thirst for news of their club. Who would be my fourth full-time boss following on in the footsteps of Kevin Keegan, Kenny Dalglish and Gullit? It would prove to be Bobby Robson and he brought with him passion, a love of the game and unflinching enthusiasm. Just what Newcastle needed in its hour of need.

Bobby made very few changes to the squad but immediately the results started to improve and slowly but surely we hauled ourselves off the bottom of the table to finish a respectable 11th by the end of the season. Just how well that almost untinkered squad has done since Gullit's departure in September 1999, goes to show how badly the Dutchman was getting things wrong. It wasn't always the players' fault as he would often have everyone believe.

He was never going to force me out from a football club and an area I have come to call home. It was a painful time but now he has gone things are once again going great for me back in the side and back, not only with a squad number, but my own number seven.

My love affair with the club is strong, stretching back to the day I was signed by Kevin Keegan in September 1992. But I'd be the first to admit that if anyone had told me during the first few days after completing my £700,000 transfer from first division Charlton Athletic to Newcastle, that I would spend the rest of my career up north then I would have laughed, or even cried, in their faces.

During those first couple of seasons up here in the north-east I would go back down south for the duration of the summer. I would have my bags packed and ready, and within hours of the final whistle on the last day of the season I would be off. But nowadays my summer plans have changed totally, it is my parents and family who come up here to see us! Myself and my wife Anna love everything about the region and its football fans. The only drawback, even now after eight years, has to be the weather – it is much colder up north!

I will always have so much to thank Kevin Keegan for. He really was the catalyst, along with the then chairman Sir John Hall, who revived a massive club from a sleeping giant to championship favourites in a few short, but wonderfully exciting, years. Everything he did for me and for the club, until things soured for him towards the very end of his five years, will go down as one of the most exciting chapters of a great club, a way of life on Tyneside.

It would take a whole book to describe the memorable times under the Keegan/Terry McDermott regime. Later in the book I will try to encapsulate just what Keegan's marvellous era at the club meant to me, no wonder the fans still call him 'The Messiah'!

As I look back there really has never been a dull moment in my 16 years in the professional game. From my first introduction to football, when my father took me along to Charlton Athletic's home ground, The Valley, where he got me a job on the turnstiles, to Newcastle's end of season tour to Trinidad and Tobago in 2000, I have hardly had time to take stock.

In that time I have played for two clubs – both very different in their make-up, but both with huge tradition. I have played for my country, at both Under-21 and full international level. I have suffered the disappointment of defeat in two FA Cup finals in consecutive seasons. However, I have also tasted great European nights, both home and away from St James', in which Newcastle defeated some of Europe's elite. Throughout the period the good times have hugely outweighed the bad. It is a career I have thoroughly enjoyed, a career I would not swap for anything.

And the fans make it even more special. I am very aware when I see the supporters trooping away after a defeat, still singing their songs in a proud, almost tribal, demonstration of intense loyalty, that I am fortunate. Having the chance to play football for such a great club is something I never wish to lose sight of or take for granted.

The Keegan years were wonderful times. Sides came to St James', a cauldron of noise, and simply tried to survive. Few, with the obvious exception of Manchester United, tried to attack us there. I often say that if we weren't ahead during those frantic opening 20 minutes or so then something was wrong. We really did have an attacking team from front to back. Kevin's only intention was to provide entertainment for, in his opinion, the best fans in the world.

How can anyone ever forget our forward line of David Ginola, Peter Beardsley, Les Ferdinand and Keith Gillespie which so nearly took us to the championship in 1995/96? And then, just to add a little much needed strength the following season, the manager went out and spent a world record fee of £15 million on England's number one – Alan Shearer.

The excitement was never ending and along with the great moments at club level came international recognition. Now 21 caps and two international goals on, I look back and treasure every minute.

Naturally, there have been moments of huge disappoint-ment along the way. Being pipped to the Premiership title in 1995/96 by an Eric Cantona-inspired Manchester United, two FA Cup final defeats and missing out on Euro 96 at the last minute when Terry Venables cut his squad down to the final 22, hurt me deeply. Then I sit back and look positively towards the future, as we look towards that elusive first major trophy for Newcastle United in decades!

But, of all those disappointments none match the empty feeling I was left with after I lost the Newcastle captaincy when Ruud Gullit so ungraciously stripped it away from me without having the decency to explain why. He must have known how much that would hurt. I dare anyone to say that they could be more proud, than I was, to carry that armband.

How life has changed for the better once again. A change of management has coincided with my return to favour and return to form. Bobby Robson has saved a few careers here, mine included. The pride is back on Tyneside again and that may not have been the case during Gullit's year-long reign. The place is transformed. The fun is back at Newcastle United. Training is great and the boss knows how to get the best out of his players.

Winning football matches and trophies has never been a question of how you look in training, and to be honest we don't work too hard in between games, it is what happens on the pitch on match day that matters to us and to the supporters who pay our wages.

Bobby has given me a new lease of life at Newcastle, for that I will always be grateful. It is so nice to prove someone wrong – to Gullit, age mattered. If you are doing the job, why should age come into the equation? Bobby Robson is the best example I can think of, aged 67 and as enthusiastic and clearly successful as ever. Long may it continue for us both!

And just think, if Sir John Hall had not installed my boyhood hero Kevin Keegan as manager I might never have moved so far north. I wouldn't have missed these experiences for the world.

When I was at my one and only other club, Charlton Athletic, I knew nothing of life up here, certainly nothing north of Watford. Of course, I knew they loved their football but not to the extent that I now know to be the case.

I remember travelling up here to Newcastle in those Division One days and feeling just how far from London it was. It was like a different country and even though I always seemed to do well against either Newcastle, Sunderland or Middlesbrough, it was in truth probably the last place I would have expected to end up at.

Charlton was a homely club where everyone knew each other and got on so well. A move to Newcastle was a massive wrench for a born-and-bred East Ender like me. But at the age of 26 it was time for me to look for pastures new.

CHAPTER TWO

TURNSTILE OPERATOR?

I was born, Robert Martin Lee, on 1 February, 1966 at Howards Road Maternity Hospital in Plaistow, East London, as it happens the year the late and great Bobby Moore of West Ham United lifted the World Cup.

I lived in a typical two-up, two-down terraced house in Edinburgh Road, Plaistow, just a stone's throw from Upton Park. No front garden, and very little back garden. And by the time I was two there were five of us – my mum, dad and brothers Mark and Dean – I was the middle one! Dad decided we needed somewhere bigger and we left the East End for the suburbs. We moved on to an estate at Gray Gardens, Rainham, Essex, about 20 minutes away from our previous terrace. This was where my early memories of childhood began.

Although the house move represented something of a new beginning, it was in many ways also a very sad time for the family as my mum's mother, Mary-Jane Davy, died at the age of 56. She was the Geordie side of my family, born in Walker Town, Jarrow in 1912. Mary-Jane was very proud of her Tyneside roots. In fact, her dad, my great granddad and brothers John and Ben walked from Jarrow to London in the great Jarrow March which took place to highlight the extreme poverty and difficulty in getting work during The Depression. Mary-Jane moved down from the north-east seeking work as a nanny in the East End which is where she met, and married, my granddad Stanley Martin, hence my middle name!

My early memories of kicking a football revolve around playing with my granddad, who bought me my very first pair of football boots. We walked all the way to the Bobby Moore Sports Shop, which was opposite the main entrance to Upton Park, to buy them. I was so proud of those boots that I walked all the way home wearing them and then rushed straight into the garden for a kickabout with my granddad. But it wasn't the greatest start to a career! I had hardly kicked my first ball before I fell flat on my face. I was rushed by ambulance to the Queen Mary Hospital in Stratford, with a lump the size of a tennis ball on my head. I was known to be injury prone in those days!

My granddad moved in with us at Gray Gardens and because he was an avid follower of the Hammers, I became one too. I think he dreamed of me playing for them one day. He was a snooker hall manager and a tick tack man at the dog tracks. Sadly, granddad passed away at the age of 68 in 1972, when I was six, but I retain great, if unfortunately too few, memories of him.

My childhood was a very happy, contented one, which I look back on with pleasure. I remember playing football in the street with my brothers and friends, something you could not possibly do now. During school holidays we would play football from dawn to dusk, stopping only when a rare passing car went across our 'pitch'. Those were happy days. We spent many hours pretending to be stars of the day like Kevin Keegan or Trevor Brooking – I was always Keegan, even when in goal! Although a Hammers fan I had a strong liking for Liverpool and Keegan in particular.

There was something about Liverpool, the Reds, at that time in the 1970s. Just as Keegan lifted the profile of Newcastle years later to the extent that you saw black and white shirts being worn by people all over the country, so he did the same for Liverpool. Like so many kids these days all over the country who support Manchester United and yet will never get the chance to watch them, I was a Liverpool fan. It was simply because they were always winning everything and they had the best player – a certain KK.

By the age of seven I was training and playing for a local Sunday morning team called Pegasus. Although at that age I was very small against the rest of the lads, most of them were nine years old, luckily even then I was quite quick and could dribble a bit! Even at this young age I was being given loads of encouragement by my family, especially my dad Reg who started taking me on runs around the block. We'd get up before he went to work, and me to school, to do this. Mind you, even at that tender age I still left him trailing behind – sorry Dad!

There is always some starting point to any life story, a moment when you feel destiny took its hold and led you to follow a certain path. Well, without any doubt in my case it was my father's Saturday afternoon job, or to be more accurate his labour of love. Monday-Friday dad had a job as a senior manager with Stolt Tank Containers but come the weekend he worked at The Valley, home of Charlton Athletic, where he was in charge of the stewards along with the people who worked on the turnstiles on match days. Unusually, because of an intense local rivalry between the clubs, he used to work for both Charlton and *Millwall*. Throughout his life, he had always supported Charlton simply because he came from Beckenham in Penge, where his family still live along with all of my cousins, and his stewarding job was just an extension of his love for the club I suppose.

So it became something of a routine for him to take me and my brothers along on match days to the ground. After all, where else could I go and play on an actual pitch where the professionals trained? In the main stand car park there was a big mound on a hill near the top corner flag, and on top of the mound there was a high fence and then inside of that there was a goal. To keep us out of mischief while he got on with his stewarding duties, dad would leave us up there playing 'World Cup' and 'three and in'. We would play our own private games as the fans walked past us, having come through the outer turnstiles on their way to the terraces where they used to stand to watch the match.

I will never forget that mound. It was maybe 20 yards high and it would cover the size of an 18 yard box. It had an old sandy goalmouth, but it has held some great memories for me. To be honest I have played on worse! I am sure it was on that mound that first team goalkeeper Nicky Johns and the others used to go and do their training. Even when I joined the club, ten years later, I would still see players going up there to do their practice.

I was reminded of that mound again only recently during Newcastle's end of season tour to Trinidad and Tobago in 2000. One of their pitches was shocking. One side of it was just dust with small craters where it had dried up, whereas the other side was all lush and green. I didn't think I would play the full game so, as captain, I chose to attack the lush area in the first half hoping to be taken off at half time so I didn't have to go back the other way! Unfortunately Bobby Robson thought differently so I spent the whole of the second half playing in the craters.

As I started to get stronger and those famous thighs began to bulge, I began to play more and more competitive football. It was becoming a way of life, my only interest at the time. Once I started Abbs Cross Secondary School, in Hornchurch, it wasn't long before I was picked to play for Havering District – a major honour. This is where I had my first encounter with a full time professional, Clive Allen. He was one of our former District stars, and had just started playing for Queens Park Rangers. He came over and joined in training with us one day.

I found school life at Abbs Cross pretty boring as the only thing that really interested me was football. Perhaps I should have paid a bit more attention – I didn't know it at the time but my future wife, Anna Steggles, was sitting two desks away from me in my class!

As a 15-year-old, dad took me along to The Valley with my friend, Peter Coyne, and got us jobs working on the turnstiles. This job gave rise to one of those stories which is so often brought up about me, namely that I'm a former turnstile operator done good! Everyone seems to think that I did the job for years, when in fact it was on only three occasions, but it has still stuck with me. That's the problem, people like the idea. In the match programmes all you see is 'former turnstile operator Rob Lee…,' which could not really be further from the truth! It is the first question I tend to get asked in interviews away from the north-east.

The 'job' had its perks – for one I was able to watch the second half of the games at The Valley once everyone had gone through into the ground. It was towards the end of the 1980/81 season and Charlton were languishing near the bottom of the second division. I had no affinity to Charlton except that my dad and my older brother Mark supported them. I am not one for breaking the law but I might as well admit that you were meant to be 16 to work on the gates, and I was only 15. In those days though there were only about 5,000 people who went through the turnstiles! Remember, this was the original Valley, a huge stadium which my dad told me used to hold 75,000 fans in the club's heydays in the 1950s.

As I said, I did this on only three occasions each time working a different turnstile, normally ticket turnstiles, but it gave me my first real taste of a professional football club – although I don't know if those early visits had any bearing on my eventual decision to sign for them. Another perk was the money: it wasn't a bad little earner for me. Fathers tended to pass their sons over the turnstile so it didn't click while I turned a blind-eye, and they would leave a fiver on the side. It was a little extra money so I didn't complain! I can't exactly remember how much I got paid – £15, maybe £20, but it seemed like a lot in those days. I think I made as much money this way as I did, a couple of years later, when the club started paying me for my duties.

Most players, certainly the older ones, had done a job before they started playing. I can think of a couple of examples. Chrissy Waddle was a former sausage maker, while Stuart Pearce was an electrician. Mind you Stu still keeps his hand in – he put up some lights at Warren Barton's house, so I'm told, so Pearcey's covered when he finally finishes playing! But the players start so young these days they don't have time to have done something else.

Naturally, in my early teenage years me and my mates were no different from other kids of that age. I tried a cigarette, but I didn't like it. I also tried alcohol, and I wasn't particularly interested in that either, but I've grown to like it! Football continued to be the focus of my existence, I was playing more and more.

My first brush with the pro game came when I began training at West Ham as a schoolboy. And it was there that I met my future manager, Alan Curbishley. I remember him as a young up and coming player in the Hammers team. He would be coaching when I used to go up to their training ground once a week. I also went to Tottenham only to be eventually discarded by Spurs, my first major setback.

I still remember the name of the guy who rejected me at Spurs. He was called Robbie Stepney and, as far as I can recall, he was a youth development officer at the club. After training at Tottenham for only three or four weeks, I played in one practice game on the left of midfield – of all places to play me. I don't know if Stepney was trying to put everyone at ease but I still remember him saying to me before the game, 'Just try and relax', but I couldn't, I was being judged and it got to me. I don't think I did particularly well, but I suppose I should be thankful that at least he came up to me after the game and told me to my face that I wasn't going to make it. 'I don't think you will make the grade,' he said. 'I don't think you are good enough'.

I will always remember that. I thought it was a bit unjust, judging me like that after just one game. So, Ruud Gullit isn't the only man to have played me out of position and then told me I wasn't in his plans! I will never forget the particular feeling of rejection, it really set me back. It's not something you want to hear at that age. I also stopped training at West Ham because I was so downbeat. Their chief scout at the time, Ronnie Gayle, tried on numerous occasions to persuade me to return but I refused. I didn't want any more heartache so I just went back to playing football with my mates. Fortunately I soon changed my mind and decided to give football another go.

The irony was that me and a couple of mates, Steve Woods and Tony Dudley, used to get driven over to Spurs by my dad because it was too far for us to go on the train. While I was kicked out, they were both kept on. So you had a situation where, even after I was rejected by a team that many years later tried to sign me, my dad was still taking my mates over to Spurs' training ground!

I often wonder what happened to Steve and Tony. In fact it's frightening really how few players make it to the top level. While I was turning out for Pegasus I played against people like Alan Kimble who is now at Wimbledon after joining them from Cambridge. There was also Terry Howard who went on to play for Leyton Orient before moving to Peterborough.

I will always remember a lad called Dave Matthews. During my teens David was the bees knees with everyone. He was an outstanding prospect. He was bigger and stronger than the rest of us and used to play for a team called River Hawks. There were rumours that West Ham were looking after him and they'd given him a few bob because they thought he was going to be their new star.

I later played against him, and West Ham, when I was in Charlton's reserves. By this stage there wasn't much between us in class. In fact I was probably better than him. A few short years can make all the difference in football. I'm not sure what happened to him in the end but he didn't make it in the pro game.

Sometimes a schoolboy starlet does make it, Tony Cottee is the prime example. When I was very young, I must have been about seven and I'd just started playing for Pegasus, we faced a team called Romford Royals. Cottee played for them. They were different class. They'd always beat us about 14–0 and Tony would score six or seven. And he's still scoring all these years on, for Norwich City.

When I think of individual players who struck a chord in my mind as I grew up, I will always go back to Mike Flanagan, the Crystal Palace striker –

he was our local hero. I went to school with his sister June, she was in the same year as me. In those days we would often just hang about and get our dinner at the local cafe. We would spot Mike and wherever he was his black sports car would be nearby, we knew it was his because it had 'Mike Flanagan – Crystal Palace FC' written along the side. We used to think, 'If only!' In our minds he was a very big soccer star. Occasionally, June would become everyone's favourite friend when she persuaded him to come over and take some coaching at Abbs Cross.

While I dreamed of becoming a footballer, earning lots of money and driving a flashy car, it was difficult to think, except when daydreaming, that I would ever really make it. It was one of those things that seemed beyond me. But, even after my early rejection by Robbie Stepney, it didn't stop me from trying to make the grade. No-one could take away my dreams. Looking back now, I admit I never used to go and watch that many games – I preferred playing – but, as West Ham were my local side, if we did go anywhere to watch a big game it was to Upton Park.

At the age of 16, my home life changed. Dad was offered the role of President of Stolt Tank Containers in Greenwich – no, not in south-east London but in Connecticut, USA, some 4,000 miles away! How inconsiderate! Of course, he wanted to take all of his family with him, but Mum did not fancy it at all. But in the end he took the job and went on his own. Ironically, as I am writing my autobiography my parents have just moved to the States for four years.

It is no exaggeration to say my dad always had, and still has, a massive influence on me and my football. In fact both mum and dad have always been right behind me in my career. She has always subscribed to The Mag, Newcastle's fanzine, and there's quite a funny story surrounding this. In the mid-1990s, when I was playing some of the best football of my career, The Mag started a campaign to get me in the England squad. They had all these T-shirts printed with a picture of my face and the slogan, 'Bobby Lee for England'. Orders started pouring in from a certain Mrs. Lee from Hornchurch, Essex. Sure enough it was mum, my number one fan! The Mag claimed she ordered 35 of them and although I know it was nothing like that many, she did buy a fair few.

But, back to my days as a teenager in Essex. Obviously, because of his new job dad wasn't around to drive me all over London and I relied instead on another early influence in my career, Ray Underhill. Ray was the manager of a team all my mates and I played for, called Sovereign, and it was indirectly through Ray that I got my big break with Charlton.

By coincidence Ray knew Martin Robinson, Charlton's left winger, very well. I kept nagging Ray to get Martin there to watch me play because I was quick to tell him what a great player I was. I obviously lacked confidence during my teens!

So one day he managed to arrange it. I have picked up many great memories while playing for my two clubs and for England but I will never forget the match 'Robbo' came to watch me play.

Before the game commenced at Valance Park, Ray announced to the rest of my team-mates, 'I want everyone to be on their best behaviour today because Robbo is coming down to watch Rob.' Naturally, I ran out and looked around for Martin. I soon spotted him as he stood at the side of the pitch. After about 20 minutes little had happened, when suddenly someone got caught with a late tackle, and it all just kicked off. It is not just in the high pressure of a top league match that tempers can really snap. A fight broke out between opposing players and then, within seconds, it seemed to have spread throughout the pitch with 21 out of 22 involved. We occasionally had the odd punch-up but nothing to match this. There were fights going on all over the pitch! In fact, there was only one player who wasn't involved in the punch-up – our goalie Colin Parker, incidentally the brother of ex-Manchester United and England defender Paul Parker.

I'm sorry to say I was heavily involved, to tell you the truth I was always involved! And when one of my mates' dads tried to break it up, he also got smacked in the face by one of our players! While all this had been going on I completely forgot about Robbo watching from the sidelines and my big chance. 'Oh god, I've blown this now!' I thought. Understandably, the match was abandoned by the referee who just happened to be our manager Ray. After things eventually simmered down and I was trudging off I remember Martin saying to me, 'Where's your next match – the Royal Albert Hall?' Once again, I thought my hopes of a career as a professional footballer were over before it had even started.

As it turned out Martin was satisfied he had seen enough in the 20 minutes of actual football for him to recommend me to the chief scout at Charlton, a lovely old boy called Les Gore.

A few weeks after I had been recommended by Robbo, Les actually came to watch me play for Sovereign. He couldn't find where we were playing, he told me much later, and turned up very late. Well, me and the lads had had more than a few sherberts the night before and after 20 minutes I went down with a bit of an injury. I thought, 'Sod this,' but Ray ran on with his magic sponge and told me, 'Rob you've got to get up, Les is here to watch you!' So I managed to pick myself up and play on.

At the time I was playing up front – which is why I started there at Charlton – and in that particular game I was playing as a centre forward. I liked to think I was the star of the show, Ray says I was, but my mates didn't agree. Anyway, Les must have seen something in me he liked because I was invited to play for a Charlton youth team a week or so later.

By the time I was 16 I was travelling to play at Charlton on a regular basis. I know the club weren't too pleased about the number of games I was playing for Sovereign and other teams, but I had my commitments! A normal weekend would go like this: I would play for Charlton's youth teams on a Saturday morning, then I had to rush back and play for Park Heath (whose players included Simon Steggles, the brother of my future wife Anna) on Saturday afternoons.

Simon and his mates were all a lot older than me, they were in their twenties, and I used to get knocked about a bit but I still enjoyed it. It probably prepared me for the rigours ahead. Then, after getting a kicking for Park Heath, I used to get up and play for Sovereign on Sunday morning as well.

With my dad having gone to work in America, it was left to Ray to take over the taxi duties, and he could not have done a better job. At the time Ray was working as a printer on the papers, getting home at six or seven o'clock in the morning, but he would always be at the house to pick me up at

8.30am to take me to the Charlton youth team games. He used to sleep in the car while the match went on. I assume it was the early starts catching up with him rather than the quality of my football!

Ray ferried me around for several months. He was a diamond and I still keep in contact with him now. If it wasn't for him I would never have been able to get to the games. Much later in life it gave me the greatest pleasure, when I returned from England duty at France '98, to give him my shirt. He never wanted anything in return for his help, but I think he was proud to receive my little gift. I will never forget how good he was.

Naturally it was Ray – who else? – who picked me up on a Saturday morning to take me to Eltham to play my first Charlton youth game. They played me at centre forward, probably because that is where I was playing for Sovereign, and I scored. Les then asked me to play for their actual Youth team, a big step up. I was delighted to do so and once again I scored. A few more youth team games followed and to be fair I was holding my own. I was then asked to play a night game for the reserves which was yet another major step up for me.

It was the first time I had played at The Valley and actually played with professional players. Kevin Dickinson, who was at Tottenham before Charlton signed him on a free, played in the game as did a few of the other older pros including Les

Berry and Terry Naylor, who was also our reserve team coach. That was my first taste at this level and I scored in the game too! I seemed to have a record of scoring on my debuts whilst at Charlton, I also scored on my first team debut.

Although I was making progress and getting regular football with the reserves and youth team it didn't seem to be leading anywhere, I felt I was beginning to lose a bit of interest. It was getting towards the end of the season, and though there were rumours that the club were going to sign me on full-time forms nothing seemed to be happening. Things came to a head when I didn't turn up one week. Les Gore was straight on the phone. 'Do you want to be a professional player?' he asked.

'Yes,' I replied, 'but I can't see it ever happening.'

He refuted this saying, 'They are going to sign you, I promise you!'

Once I heard this it raised my spirits and ended the doubts I was having.

I have a lot to be grateful to Les for. Sadly, he is no longer with us. He died while I was still at Charlton, a very sad day three or four years before I moved on to Newcastle. One of my greatest regrets is that Les didn't see me go on to play for England and captain my club at Wembley.

The season ended and in the summer of 1983 I went down to the ground with Les and signed a one-year contract with the club. Manager Lennie Lawrence wasn't there, nor were there any press and television crews to capture my big moment. It was a case of in, sign the forms with his assistant Eddie May, and out – what a difference to when I signed my first deal with Newcastle United nearly nine years later. It was only a 12-month contract and, in fact, I had been getting more money doing my previous job as a shipping clerk at Stolt. My first salary at Charlton earned me the huge sum of £110 a week. Wow! Surely now it would all be plain sailing, nothing could possibly go wrong … could it? I was finally through the door at Charlton.

I am often asked why I wasn't signed as an apprentice. The fact was that you had to do a two-year apprenticeship, which was between the ages of 16 to 18. As I was 17, I was half way through already and so too old! Where was I to hear that again? But at least it got me out of most of the dirtier jobs apprentices used to have to do, but unfortunately not all of them. For instance I didn't have to clean the toilets, paint the rickety old stands, or clean the professionals' boots. Mind you, I still knew my place. I wasn't allowed to go into the first team dressing room, unless invited – how things have changed, for the worst in my opinion. In my day the young players were in awe of all the pros, scared even, and certainly wouldn't speak to them unless spoken to first.

Back on the pitch things continued to go well. I was scoring quite a few goals for the reserves who were now coached by former West Ham defender Tommy Taylor, the current Leyton Orient boss. I enjoyed working with Tommy. He helped me a great deal in those early formative days giving me huge encouragement – he certainly believed in me. I can still remember him saying to me at the time, 'If you work hard, work on your first touch' – it was like a trampoline at the time – 'you can be the best player at the club.'

However, Tommy was by no means a pushover and when we played badly he certainly let us know! On more than one occasion he'd bring boxing gloves in and, in a bid to toughen us up, would take us into the gym and make us spar for a couple of rounds. Tommy certainly wasn't a small bloke so you can guess I've never forgotten those times, a few of the lads even ended up with bloody noses.

On another of those infamous occasions, Tommy brought a rugby ball in. This time the lads found themselves covered in mud and, again, a few bloody noses to remember the session by. Great times, great bloke – cheers Tom! I can also recall an incident in which we lost a game he thought we should have won. He soon had us running up and down the terraces and, I promise you, the terraces at Charlton were a long way up! Tommy was tough but he was also good fun.

If the training for us was tough, it was still nothing compared to the massive problems the club was facing financially at the time. In fact, before I had the opportunity to make my debut for the first team the club went into liquidation. They were worrying times for the club, and the players, on more than one occasion, would find our wages weeks late.

Before I joined the club there was even a story of Alan Simonsen, the former European Player of the Year who amazingly signed for little Charlton from Barcelona, refusing to board a team bus to an away game unless he was paid immediately. I think they paid him, but he had had enough and left the club soon afterwards. I believe Charlton had hoped to copy what Newcastle did around the same time – the Geordies pulled in the crowds by signing a huge star of the game, in their case Kevin Keegan. But unfortunately, Simonsen didn't have the pulling power of a certain Special K.

With mounting financial problems it was clear things were coming to a head, we were going under and the receivers were on their way. Then, at the last minute we were saved by Sunley – a well known building firm luckily run by a great old Charlton fan, John Fryer. Then Jimmy Hill came onto the board and not long after Sunley took over the running of the club. I came in and played in the first game at home to Grimsby Town under the new regime. So, from thinking I was going to be out of a job I was making my first team debut in a matter of days. As they say, football's a funny game.

I can remember my debut as though it was yesterday, the date was 10 March, 1984. I played up front alongside Charlton legend Derek Hales and Martin Robinson, Robbo being the guy who recommended me. In actual fact it was Robbo who put me through to score my debut goal for the first team! Some help he proved to be during those early days of my professional career! I broke through the Grimsby defence and finished with a low right foot drive into the bottom corner. The final score was 3–3, a six-goal thriller watched by a massive crowd of 7,626. My debut had come and gone in a blink of an eye – how time flies when you are having fun.

I was quickly brought back down to earth by being left out of the side for the next game, an away match at Brunton Park, Carlisle. Just after half time we found ourselves 3–0 down. The fans started chanting for Lennie Lawrence to bring me on but he turned to me and said, 'I'm not putting you on, the lads have been crap, they can get themselves out of it!' The game finished 3–0, the first defeat of my career. We experienced much happier times in Carlisle two seasons later when we clinched promotion to the old first division at Brunton Park, winning 3–2.

Things were so different in those days when we were regularly watched by 5-6,000. Older fans, who remembered massive crowds of 75,000 in late 1940s and 1950s, knew that Charlton had been one of the biggest clubs around, but in my time cash was always very tight. I think I joined professional football when it was in a bit of a mess financially. And you know, at that time, they used to say that too much football on telly was driving the crowds away. People in general were scratching their heads not knowing what was to become of the game. And the crowds in most instances were poor.

With us only pulling in around 5,000 supporters we relied a great deal on the loyalty of our fans. An example of this was when we wanted to buy Ronnie Moore, who is now manager of Rotherham, but at the time was a powerful centre-forward with an eye for goal. Our fans helped to buy him by standing around the ground with collection buckets. Most fans chipped in. I think the fee was £17,000.

Things were much simpler in those days. It was quite common to travel on the coach to places like Newcastle and Sunderland back then, whereas of course now everybody flies.

So it is great to see a club like Charlton, who had entertained huge crowds in the past at The Valley, well on the way to once again regaining a large following. Nowadays the 'sold-out' signs go up every week as Alan Curbishley's side provide such great entertainment for the fans. How times have changed from those dark days in the eighties.

We were forced to move away from The Valley in September 1985 because of the state of the stadium. I remember that during my second season in the first team the huge open side was condemned and we weren't allowed to have anybody in there, so we played to a three-sided stadium. We had to leave and eventually ended up at Selhurst Park, the home of Crystal Palace.

Football was still very much a learning curve for me but one game I will never forget was a second division clash with Portsmouth during my first season. We played Pompey at home and Lennie came to me before the game looking a little worried.

'How are you feeling?' he said.

I told him I was okay.

'You're not getting tired or anything? I'm thinking of resting you.'

I said that I didn't want to be rested.

Anyway he trusted my word, he left me in and I scored two goals. We beat Portsmouth 2–1.

It was a very good decision by the manager!

During the last ten games of my first season in 1983/84 I scored four goals. Out of those games the one that sticks in my memory the most was the one against Newcastle United and yes, you've guessed it, Kevin Keegan. It was to be his last game in

London. I was actually going to get the opportunity to play against my childhood hero! I couldn't wait! But Keegan wasn't the only star. They also had Terry McDermott (who was to become Keegan's trusted assistant at Newcastle), Chris Waddle and Peter Beardsley (who was proving such a young star alongside his mentor Keegan). We lost 3–1 after taking an early lead but the game just passed me by.

It is not an exaggeration to say I was in absolute awe of Keegan even though he was coming to the end of his playing career.

I started my first full season with Charlton in August 1984 with an away game at Cardiff, which we won comfortably 3–0, Derek Hales getting a hat-trick. In fact we made a great start to the season, I think we were about second in the league after the opening dozen or so games. And if my memory is right, Hales had scored 13 goals while I had fired precisely 13 less! I really was running my socks off for the team while he was scoring goals for fun and picking up the headlines.

After the fine start, Charlton as usual came down to earth with a bang in the New Year – along with the Christmas decorations. We had a real struggle after that. Obviously, as I was still adjusting to the pace of things it meant I was occasionally left out of a few games and then I would be put back again – 'Resting you', I think they call it.

Going back to Derek Hales, he was a larger than life character with his bushy beard and even bushier head of hair. He looked as if he had just come from the fairground to play, boy he looked hard! During that first full season of playing up front with him, I had to take more than a few elbows and whacks from over robust defenders. Remember, there was no Sky Television to catch them out in those days. Somebody would be giving me a hard time so Derek would do the 'switch with me sign,' and then the fun would begin – generally one way. The next time there was a challenge it was inevitable that it wasn't 'Halesy' who ended up in a heap on the floor. He was a very respected hard man, and no-one messed with him.

Derek was like a minder to me and he was very, very good at this. He wasn't a bad striker either! He used to stick in a few goals in his time. He'd be there scoring and then the next minute he'd be sorting out a few defenders.

I also got on very well with Derek off the pitch. He was one from the old school. He liked to drink, played hard both on and off the field. Some days he would arrive at The Valley with shotguns under his arms and help the club out by shooting down pigeons from under the roof of the stand. Derek also had a taxi firm and he would arrive on match days in his cab.

He was a great character and couldn't do

enough to help me out during those early appearances. I was fortunate that I got on with him and had his respect, but I suppose if he didn't like you then you were in trouble. It wasn't unknown for him to come in to training more than a little worse for wear. He did turn up late for training on a few occasions. Derek was very difficult to control, but I respected him.

My relationship with Lennie was generally very good. He used to keep a close eye over us, like a school master, but I liked him. He was straight to the point and always with an answer. However, I still had my ups and downs with the boss – like on the, not too numerous, occasions he decided to leave me out. One time he approached me and told me I was being 'rested' for the forthcoming game. Of course, I was very unhappy with this decision and told him so.

'Why boss? There are other players playing worse than me – Andy Peake for one!'

He stopped me dead when, quick as a flash, he answered, 'I know, I am seeing him next.'

After many years of disappointment I sensed that Charlton's fortunes might be turning. For the start of the 1985/86 season the club amazingly spent almost £500,000 on six players – John Pearson, John Humphrey, John Pender, George Shipley, Mark Reid and Steve Thompson. Were we really going for promotion? We certainly were!

And as I've said, we clinched promotion to the old First Division (now Premier League) at Brunton Park with a game to spare!

What followed were four years of a constant struggle to stay with the elite of the English game, but four enjoyable years all the same.

CHAPTER THREE

LIFE AT THE VALLEY

Most of the memories I carry around with me of my time at Charlton, surround the team's attempts to stay in the then old first division. Our first season, 1986/87, was a long hard struggle, finishing with us being dragged into a play-off with three teams from the second division and ourselves fighting it out to stay in the top flight.

We disposed of Ipswich Town in the two-legged semi-final and faced Leeds United for the right to play in the first division the following season. We played Leeds at home first with Jim Melrose scoring the only goal in our 1–0 victory.

With Leeds winning the away game by the same margin it went into a third and final decider to be played on a neutral ground – St Andrews, the home of Birmingham City. While we didn't have a big fan base the Yorkshiremen had massive support. After 90 minutes the game was still locked at 0–0. Then, after a few minutes of extra time we found ourselves 1–0 down. I thought, as many of our fans did, that we were heading back to the second division, from which we'd only just gained promotion after almost 30 years. Then our centre back Peter Shirtliff came up from the back to score firstly the equaliser and then the goal which was to prove the winner. Unbelievably, we were still in the big league.

The following season we were almost dragged into it once again. In the final game of the season we had to go to another hostile ground – Stamford Bridge – to face Chelsea. We needed a draw and Chelsea needed a victory in order to avoid the play-offs. Chelsea took an early lead but our experienced ex-Tottenham defender Paul Miller scored with a deflected shot. Once again we had forced the result we needed. Incidentally, Chelsea went into the play-offs instead of us and were relegated. What an atmosphere there was at the Bridge that day.

Certain clubs always seem to produce an atmosphere unique to them. Millwall is certainly one of those clubs. I remember several years later in the 1992/93 season early in my Newcastle career, we had to visit the infamous Cold Blow Lane for a promotion game against the Lions. What an atmosphere it was that day, one of the most hostile ever, but we kept our nerve and came away with a 2–1 victory thanks to goals from Andy Cole and Lee Clark.

Some managers would not allow their players to get intimidated by such hostile environments. The best example I can remember concerned the great Brian Clough. I remember Stuart Pearce telling me that one year Clough, before his Nottingham Forest team were due to face Millwall at The Den, made his team leave the sanctuary of the team bus half a mile from their original stadium and walk to Cold Blow Lane just to show they were not scared of them. I don't usually get intimidated but I wouldn't have fancied that!

During the happier times at The Valley I used to love playing against all three sides from the north-east – Newcastle, Sunderland and Middlesbrough – because it felt as if I used to score goals there all the time. I remember one occasion in particular because it threw up a really funny tale. It was a midweek evening game in the old first division and it was pissing down with rain. We faced Newcastle United at St James' and there were 20,000 or so mad Geordies watching. Well, in this game we were storming, we really were flying, and we were comfortably 3–0 up before Kevin Brock got one back in the end.

At the time Newcastle were rumoured to be interested in our right back John Humphrey who was playing brilliantly for us. He really was the main man. There were stories splashed over the back of many newspapers indicating Newcastle were ready to offer half a million quid or whatever for him. I remember him saying to me in the shower after the game, 'Tell you what mate, even I couldn't save this club.' Of course it was a bit tongue in cheek, but how things were soon to change up on Tyneside. I never for one moment thought that it would be me, and not John, who would eventually be part of the Geordie Revolution.

John was so funny, a hilarious guy! On another occasion QPR were rumoured to be interested in him and he was granted permission to speak to Trevor Francis, the then Loftus Road manager. John went to his house to discuss terms and had a picture taken shaking hands with Trevor. The deal eventually broke down but not before John, on returning to Charlton, thought it would be absolutely hilarious to stick the photo under Lennie's office door. All we heard were swear words and then a big roar of laughter from Lennie who quickly saw the funny side. He could always take a joke even when under pressure, which he normally was.

A good example of this was when we were struggling in our usual position at the foot of the first division and Lennie was rumoured to be close to the sack. A group of us were sitting at the dining table and Lennie came in with a long face.

'Things are looking bad lads,' he said. 'We lost again Saturday, I'm close to the sack and my greyhound lost last night!'

Typically, John Humphrey came back with, 'And the press officer's shagging your missus!'

'I said things were bad, not suicidal,' said Lennie.

Times were generally hard for Charlton, constantly fighting for survival in the first division. The 1988/89 season proved to be our best. After signing a few good experienced players like Colin Pates and Joe McLaughlin from Chelsea we finished 14th! It may not seem like a great feat to many but for a club the size of Charlton, with not much money and still playing every game away from home at Selhurst Park, I consider it quite an achievement. But it was not to last. The following season, 1989/90, we finished 19th and there was no escape hatch – we were relegated this time!

Relegation signalled a new, unwelcome, period for the club, but there was also a change for me personally, for the better. I had played right winger during my four years in the first division but for the start of the 1990/91 season Lennie decided to play me in a new position, a free role allowing me to roam all over the pitch. I loved it and it really suited the team. I managed to score 13 goals and we just missed out on the play-offs.

Ultimately though Lennie couldn't get us back to the top flight so, for the start of the 1991/92 season there was a new regime in place, a double-headed management team. Lennie left for Middlesbrough and Steve Gritt and Alan Curbishley took over the reins.

I found myself back on the wing, and playing our home games at Upton Park! Whether the club found the rent or the rates too high at Selhurst Park I don't know, or perhaps it was Alan Curbishley's connections at West Ham, but the club was on the move again. It may not have suited our long suffering fans but it suited me on two fronts. Firstly, it was closer to my home and secondly and more importantly, I was going to get to play at the famous Boleyn Ground on a regular basis, even if it was not to be in the famous claret and blue!

However, as the 1992/93 season approached I found myself having thoughts about moving on and trying something different, a feeling I had never had before. There were rumours about different clubs. Tottenham and Everton were mentioned and also Derby County.

I spoke to Steve and Alan on numerous occasions and they were very understanding. Partly, because I was in the last year of my contract and partly because the club was in dire financial difficulties anyway! I felt that at the age of 25 going on for 26 if I didn't go then I would never actually go at all. I felt I'd never know how good I could have been.

Contrary to the belief that Charlton's need for cash in the end pushed me out, I have to say that they did not try to push me or force me to stay. Anyway, as I showed in my later troubles with Ruud Gullit seven years on there was no forcing me. I think all three of us, Steve, Alan and myself, knew that I was going to go, it was just a question of where! They knew I had a preference for West Ham, being a life long supporter and as Alan knew the West Ham manager, Billy Bonds, very well he said he would keep him informed about my impending transfer.

Obviously, I still spoke regularly to a former team-mate of mine, Andy Peake, who was then captain of Middlesbrough – Lennie Lawrence had taken Andy with him to Ayresome Park. Andy told me that Boro were very interested in me, but when the Charlton management team called me into the office one morning before training I didn't really know who it was coming in for me. Steve and Alan pulled me in and said, 'Lennie's on the phone and he wants to speak to you. We have agreed a fee of £700,000.'

I spoke to Lennie and he said he wanted me to come up to Ayresome Park and speak to him. My mind was in a whirl, I hadn't even thought about Middlesbrough until that moment. It was the first time I'd actually been able to speak to another manager and I admit now it was a strange feeling despite the fact that I knew Lennie well. But I agreed to go and speak to him.

As a transfer was now very much on the cards I knew now was the time to see if West Ham were prepared to come in for me. I put the phone down and immediately spoke to Alan.

'Are you going to contact Billy?' I asked.

'He'll probably be out training at the moment so I can't, I will try later,' he said. I still don't know whether he did or not. He rang me after I had signed for Newcastle to explain his reason, which was that West Ham had only offered half a million pounds for me at the time and would not match the £700,000 offered by the two other clubs, Middlesbrough and Newcastle. Alan said that he was under strict instructions and he couldn't tell me of their interest, the club fearing that I would turn down the two northern clubs and wait for my boyhood favourites to come in for me. I believe Alan could have helped me more but I certainly bear no grudges against him.

I flew up to meet Lennie that same afternoon with my dad who was back from the States. We met Lennie at Ayresome Park and spent a good few hours talking about the plans he had for me and Middlesbrough. We agreed the financial package without too many problems but I still had my doubts. I told Lennie that I would go home and speak to my family over the next few days and give him a decision then.

We went back to the hotel where we were staying for the night in Middlesbrough to be met by Andy Peake. He took us for a meal and tried his best to persuade me to sign. I was still unsure.

The next few days were spent trying to decide what was going to be best for my career and more importantly my family. Anna had recently given birth to our first child, Oliver, and a move so far north would obviously have been a major upheaval for us all. I spoke again to Lennie on the phone and agreed to meet him with Anna in London on the Friday evening.

I think Lennie, who knew me very well, realised I was having major doubts about leaving London. Just before I was due to leave I had a phone call – it was Alan Curbishley. 'Another club has come in for you!' he said. My thoughts immediately were of West Ham.

'Who is it?' I asked him.

'It is Kevin Keegan at Newcastle'.

The rest, as they say, is history.

As I've already mentioned, a lot has been made of my getting Charlton out of financial trouble, that my fee helped the club get back to The Valley. I don't know if that was true but what was disappointing at the time I left was that they were at the top of the table. Newcastle were second, behind them, and yet all of a sudden they had to sell me to their nearest rivals, something which must have angered our joint managers.

It wasn't that I had lost my feelings for the club, that's rubbish as anyone who knew me there knows, it was simply time for pastures new. But I wouldn't have gone just anywhere. I think I proved that because I ended up at St James' and didn't go to the first club to make a serious bid for me, namely Lennie Lawrence at Middlesbrough.

I make no qualms about it, the only reason I spoke to Newcastle was because of Kevin Keegan. That was the sole reason! And I said so when I joined. For instance, I have a great deal of respect for former Newcastle managers such as Jim Smith and Ossie Ardiles, and many others, but I would never even have spoken to them never mind signed.

Derby County boss Arthur Cox, who incidentally took Keegan to Newcastle as a player and has retained a great relationship with the now England coach, came in for me the year before I moved. I believe he offered Gary Micklewhite in a player exchange but Charlton wanted straight cash. In the end I only spoke to two clubs: one was a Premier League club, Middlesbrough, whose manager I knew so well; and the other, I knew nothing about except that Kevin Keegan was very much in charge. In the end that was enough for me.

I have picked up some accolades during my career but nothing has made me feel more proud than an award handed to me by the Charlton fans.

They voted for their best ever players a little while ago and I was high on that list. I remember their Hall of Fame and the past legends of many great Charlton years, so to be included in that list makes me very proud indeed.

I finished third in their voting for the all-time Charlton greatest player, behind the legendary Sam Bartram and Derek Hales. They commissioned a poster which an artist did of me. You can guess just how I was made to feel, to be thought of as one of the legends of Charlton. I am genuinely very proud of this accolade especially as it was the club my dad has always supported.

Charlton were, and are, a very homely club and they haven't gone for being corporate. They are still small enough to be a fans club but, as they have proven, big enough to be in the Premier League. I don't think they would take it as a slight if I said that they will never be one of the biggest, but they've certainly come a long way since I was there.

I often wonder why it was two clubs from the same region who were so desperate to sign me, maybe it was my performances up in the north-east for Charlton over the years which had struck a chord. I even remember receiving, on a couple of occasions, cut glass for Man of the Match performances at Roker Park from Sunderland chairman Bob Murray. Those performances may well have led to the move to Newcastle and all that would entail. Maybe I was destined to make the reverse trip to the one made by my grandmother half a century earlier.

CHAPTER FOUR

FROM ROBIN TO MAGPIE

Kevin Keegan was, of course, my biggest hero in football, but so too was Terry McDermott. They had both starred in Liverpool's domination of domestic and European football in the late 1970s and early 1980s. He had since joined up with Kevin again at Newcastle as his right-hand man, a perfect choice as he so often took the pressure off the United boss with his joking and relaxed nature.

So it did Newcastle's chances no harm to have him alongside Kevin when the Magpies swooped for me in September 1992.

I was told by Charlton to call up Terry Mac, so I did, and he got straight to the point. 'Just speak to Kevin,' said Terry, 'just give him five minutes.'

'I don't think it will make much difference. I've almost made my mind up,' I told him.

But he was insistent. 'He'll ring you in five minutes, just speak to him.'

As Terry had promised, Kevin rang up exactly five minutes later, I found he was always punctual. As soon as I heard him on the phone, I must confess I started to lose it a bit. It was all a bit much. This was *Kevin Keegan*, my boyhood hero ringing me. 'Hello this is Kevin Keegan', he began and from then on I didn't hear anything else that he said. Sorry Kev!

I probably didn't sound very enthusiastic to Kevin, I said, 'I'm not sure that I want to come to Newcastle.' I just didn't want to put all my cards on the table. In my heart I still wasn't sure I wanted to leave London.

But Kevin's got a very persuasive manner. 'Just come up and speak to me, and see the ground,' he said. Straight away he seemed confident, and within minutes he was telling me where he wanted me to play in his side.

'You're the player I want,' he said. 'If I don't get you I'll get someone similar to you, but you're my number one target. Look, think about it over the weekend and I'll ring you Sunday night at six o'clock and you can let me know then.'

I thought about nothing else. That weekend I think Newcastle went and won 5–0 against Bristol

City and the player I was meant to be replacing, Franz Carr, scored and played well by all accounts. After that performance I thought maybe Keegan wouldn't ring, but six o'clock on the dot the telephone rang and I knew who it would be on the other end. 'Yes,' I said, 'I'll come and speak to you.'

Anyway, I travelled up to Newcastle and spoke to Kevin. We didn't get off to the best start. Anna was wearing something red, not realising about the rivalry between Newcastle and Sunderland, and Kevin gave her a bit of stick. After we had met him he showed us around St James'. I will never forget the weather that day, it was raining, drizzly and grey.

Incredibly, he said he had arranged a press conference to announce my signing at 4 o'clock! Then he added, 'If you don't agree with anything, you can always call it all off.' My adviser at the time was John Hollins and he had no doubts, he thought it was a good move for me. And in truth, I was more sure of this move than I was with a move to Middlesbrough. I saw the ground at Newcastle, which was massive, and obviously I was taken by the fact that Kevin Keegan himself had come to meet us and shown us around the place.

Having grown up following Liverpool as well as my local Hammers team, I was a massive fan of Keegan's – something he told me he knew after I signed. He went on to say in his autobiography he thought that would give him a distinctive advantage over the other clubs rumoured to be interested in signing me – and it was true.

He also claims in his book that he hoodwinked me into signing for him by telling me that Newcastle was closer to London than Middlesbrough. And he takes great satisfaction from telling everyone that I was daft enough to believe it! But that is not strictly true – I had done geography at school! What he actually said was, 'Basically you don't want to go to Boro because Newcastle is a lot closer to London.' When I asked him what he meant by that he said, 'Stick you in the middle of Newcastle and you'll be down in London quicker. There's more planes and trains because it is a bigger city.'

After I signed there were loads of rumours flying around the game that I'd gone to Tyneside simply because Newcastle had offered me much better terms than Middlesbrough, and could pay me in cash and all sorts of silly stuff like that. It is all rubbish! I signed for Newcastle for less than I was offered at Middlesbrough, so it certainly wasn't the money! All Newcastle did was match their offer to Charlton.

The club made me feel very welcome and they even arranged for their chairman Sir John Hall to meet me later that afternoon at the press conference. And I remember that he was excellent – he was such an impressive man.

Although the deal was now agreed there were a few outstanding problems with Charlton. The main thing was they owed me some loyalty bonus. It was only a few grand, hardly a massive amount, but it was a matter of principle. 'I won't sign without it', I said. After all, I had been there nine years and they were refusing me my loyalty bonus which I was due.

Charlton were digging their heels in over it so Keegan got on the phone to Roger Alwin, the then chairman. 'Is that Roger? It is Kevin Keegan here.' Roger must have got the same shock that I got when he rang me. He'd probably never spoken to anybody like Keegan before but he was soon to find out, as I did, how persuasive he could be.

Keegan said, 'He's been with you nine years, shown you great loyalty. He's been brilliant for your club, and you've got £700,000 from this deal and yet you're refusing him monies he is due.' Straight after the phone call it was settled within a minute, no problem!

I would have signed anyway, to be honest, even if that hadn't happened, it was just the principle of the thing that really annoyed me.

Kevin was great from the off, he had always been my hero and he never disappointed me. It's like when you idolise someone for so long, sometimes when you meet them it can be a major disappointment, but he was all the things you can imagine a hero to be as a boy. He was all that, and more.

Some of these so called legends that you meet are not such nice people as you might think. There's no doubt Ruud Gullit, for instance, was a truly great player, like Keegan, but as people you just cannot compare them, they are like chalk and cheese. While Keegan would talk to anyone, Gullit had trouble communicating with his players never mind anyone else.

While I talk about former managers at Newcastle, Kenny Dalglish was very different to both of the others. Well, he was in public anyway, but behind the scenes he was exactly the same as Kevin. To me he was a legend, even though some might call him a bit surly.

But no-one can inspire you like Keegan could in the dressing room before we went out. He made you feel ten feet tall, no matter who you were. I remember one game in par-ticular, it must have been quite early in my Newcastle career.

We were about to play Man United at home, I had been struggling with an injury to my left leg and I was pulled in for a late fitness test. I was having trouble running it off in the warm-up, and by the time I'd got back into the dressing room I assumed I wouldn't be playing. By now all the players had run out and it was just me left there with our physio, Derek Wright. Moments later

Keegan came in, shut the door and spoke to Derek.

'How is he?'

'Not good boss,' said Derek, 'the left leg's giving him trouble.'

'Well,' said Keegan simply, 'don't kick with it!'

Me and Derek just looked at each other in amazement. There was a bit of a stunned silence. Kevin was obviously waiting for an answer.

'Well...' he continued, looking at Derek again, 'will Rob be alright if he doesn't kick with it?'

'Um ... er ... I suppose so,' he replied.

'Well that's settled then,' said Keegan. 'I want you to play, the fans want you to play and the players want you to play, so get out there and show them!'

So, I played, and played quite well as it happens. We drew 1–1 and I set up our goal for Andy Cole with a nice cross (with my *right* foot, of course.)

But that's the sort of thing Kevin could do for you. He is such an incredible motivator. Because he was always so confident, and full of beans, his mood rubbed off on the players. He made us think we could do anything. It was a brilliant environment to be in.

I'm sure the strength of Kevin's personality persuaded many of his future players to sign. As far as I was concerned, if you were for sale and you spoke to Kevin, then you signed. Simple as that. He's got such a tremendous aura about him. I was already on the verge of turning down Lennie because Middlesbrough was too far north, and within a week I'd signed for their north-east neighbours! And it was all down to Kevin. I think it was the same with Alan Shearer. He had his pick of ten of the best clubs in the world after Euro 96, but he signed for Newcastle. Les Ferdinand was another example. Kevin is so charismatic. He made you feel wanted, really part of the set-up and his mood was infectious.

But he really made me the player I hope I am today. I was probably an average first division player when I went to Newcastle – KK made me into an international player. He changed the position I played to benefit both myself and the team. After only a week at Newcastle he said, 'You can play for England. If you want to then I believe you can'. It was a wonderful thing to be told, a great boost, although at the time I thought, 'I bet he says that to everybody!'

One thing I will never forget is Kevin telling me when I signed, 'The fans bought you. The fans coming through the gate have generated the money and managed to buy you, Rob.' Hopefully, I've been a good investment! He was later quoted as saying that I was the best value for money signing he made during his five years in charge. My answer to that is simple. It's because I was so cheap!

To be fair Kevin could see that I was being wasted

on the wing. So he played me up front, then he played me just behind the front two, and then in midfield. In fact, he played me all over. Then me and Lee Clark used to rotate. And when we were under a bit of pressure Gavin Peacock would also play in midfield.

For my first game on 23 September 1992, I was a little nervous to say the least. I arrived at St. James' an hour before kick-off having not met any of my new team-mates and was thrown straight into the starting line up for the Coca-Cola Cup, second round tie against, of all teams Middlesborough, the club I had publicly turned down for being too far north! I remember the first pass of the match from Liam O'Brien which the Republic of Ireland midfielder pinged out to me on the flank. It came at me like an exocet missile, I thought, 'Shit, I'd better control this properly, or else it could be the end of my career before it starts.'

Luckily enough I did. The rest of the game was uneventful really and I came off after 75 minutes mentally and physically drained. After the game I went into the players bar to meet my good friend Andy Peake who was playing for Boro. I was standing with 'Peaky' and a few Boro players, who I'd met when visiting Ayresome Park just weeks earlier, when suddenly they all started to leave to board their coach home. There I was, pint in hand, all alone thinking maybe, just maybe I had joined the wrong club. Luckily that feeling didn't stay with me for too long.

My first league game was against Peterborough at London Road and this was really when I began to appreciate the level of support Newcastle get from the fans. The travelling Toon Army is an incredible sight. I think we took about 8-9,000 with us that day. Compare this with the 4-5,000 that we attracted at Charlton, and that was for home games! The Geordie supporters took over the whole of Peterborough and the kick-off was delayed just to find areas of the stadium to fit them all in! My parents travelled up from Essex to see the match and they couldn't stop talking about the sheer number of fans. That was the moment I realised what a massive club I had joined.

That first away game almost saw me in major trouble, along with my room-mate John Beresford. I was supposed to room with Mick Quinn and 'Bez' with Kevin Brock but Bez and I got on so well that we soon swapped and roomed together for years. Anyway, John loved a bit of a flutter and on the morning of the game he suggested we go into town to have a bet on the matches being played that afternoon. I just went along for the ride, really. I'd never done it before.

I didn't realise you were allowed to clear off into town on the morning of a game but Bez said it was fine as long as we made it back for the team meeting by a certain time. We put the bets on and had a bit of a stroll round, but then we couldn't find a cab to get us back to the hotel. The team meeting was getting closer and closer and I thought, 'Oh great, Keegan will be well happy with this, late for my first team meeting!' Then, just as we were giving up hope this bloke, who'd been in the bookies, offered us a lift. We jumped in and got back to the hotel in the nick of time.

As for the game we beat them 1–0 with a goal from Kevin Sheedy to extend our winning run. I got off to a decent start rather than a dynamic one.

For the first year or so while I settled, I was up and down the A1 more times than members of the AA. Oliver, our eldest son, was only fourteen months and my wife had never been away from home either. So, until I had settled we decided that they would remain down south. Sometimes I used to leave London at 10 o'clock at night, arrive at Durham for 2am, grab a few hours' sleep and then be up for training at 10am.

The ironic thing was that, on the rare occasions that I stayed in the north-east, I would always stay with Peaky and his family on an estate not far from, yes you've guessed it, Middlesbrough. There I was, Newcastle's newest signing, after turning down Boro, staying in Middlesbrough! Weird or what.

Perhaps because Anna didn't move up to join me straight away there have continued to be rumours that we weren't settled up here. It's been said that we hated it in the north-east, made few friends and were desperate to move back down south. It is absolute rubbish! We've had it every single year. Probably last year, when I truly was on the verge of leaving the club, under Ruud Gullit, was the only time it was justified. And even then they were saying it was cut and dried that I'd be going to Fulham, or even back to Charlton.

It was simply not true. I repeat I was not unhappy in the north-east, I loved it. The city is full of restaurants and clubs and there's plenty to do. Compared to London, parking's no problem at all and I always feel safe up here at night, which is not always the case down south. Anna moved up here within a month. Obviously she didn't stay up here all the time. There was no real need as the kids weren't yet in school. I found a house as quickly as I could, in Durham City which we rented. It was a big old house with a big garden, but it was very cold. We stayed there for just over a year, until we purchased our first home.

It is true though, as I've said, that every summer I went back down south to be with the family. As soon as the season was over that was it, we were in the car and away. Because of this I never went away on any end of season trips. Before the last game, my bags were all packed, all in the car and then I'd go straight back down to London. We would stay down all summer and come back the day before pre-season training commenced.

That was how I did it for the first year or two. But gradually it happened less and less. Then the kids started school and I started travelling with the England squad during the summer which obviously cut it down even further.

Our family came up here quite a lot and stayed with us, and they enjoyed it here. Once the kids were in school we couldn't keep taking them out the whole time. But, while some people are able to settle very quickly wherever they go, in truth it took me at least a year and a half to really settle and feel part of it.

However, I still had that feeling in the back of my mind that maybe I'd be up here a couple of years and then I'd move back to a club in London. I certainly didn't expect to stay here this long, but how things change and quite clearly now we are really settled here as a family and genuinely think of it as home.

It is important that I put the record straight about my contract and what many people for years have thought it included. There were no clauses stating that if I was unhappy I could just use that as an excuse to leave. When you have a man like Kevin Keegan, with his man-management skills you know he will look after you. So I rented for the first year and then I signed another contract. After 18 months Keegan came to me and said, 'I want you to sign again. But if you're not happy and you want to go back to London I will not stand in your way Rob.'

Immediately, stories started appearing stating that I had a clause in my contract which said if I was not happy I could leave at any time. I could, that is correct, but neither party, either me or the club, suggested it was written into my contract. However, I did have a verbal agreement with Kevin. I didn't have any such clause, and would never have asked for one.

Kevin's man-management skills are famous, he seems to know how to talk with anyone from the youngest fan to well-known people like the Sultan of Brunei. He is able to put anyone at ease and is genuinely interested in what they have to say. Despite his shock departure from St James' in January 1997 he has stayed up in the north-east as – he loves it up here.

I will always remember his warmth when I first came up to sign. He went out of his way to make me and my family feel at home. Nothing was too much trouble. Anna and I met him and his wife Jean for lunch. And I remember our son Oliver climbing all over Jean. I thought, 'There goes my little terror making a nuisance of himself all over the boss's wife.' The following day Kevin took us house hunting in his car. Kevin put Oliver's seat in the back and drove us round many of the nicest areas, including Darras Hall, Ponteland and Durham.

He was sitting in the front eating his midget gems, little wine gums, and showing us all the areas which he felt we would be interested in moving to, that was simply brilliant and something we will never forget.

And it wasn't just our family Kevin looked after and showed genuine interest in. There was a great moment, not long after I arrived, which illustrates how caring the club is. In fact this story became a running joke. One day I told Kevin that I had a dog. I think Kevin kept telling the chairman, as a joke, that my dog was unhappy and it might make me want to go back south. Well, the chairman used to have a massive party for the club staff at his house every year, it was held more often than not in his conservatory – which most of the club fitted in, it was so big. In the middle of the party he called me up in front of everybody and gave me this present of a huge bone. 'I hope this keeps your dog happy,' he said.

That is the kind of care and attention which Kevin and Sir John used to show us the players.

Needless to say, our dog, Gemma, wanted to stay here. She's still chewing the bone now!

It wasn't just on the management side where everyone made my family feel welcome, the players were also brilliant. At the time there were people like Kevin Scott, David Kelly, John Beresford and Barry Venison. I enjoyed their company because the dressing room wasn't cliquey at all. Consequently, my wife and I were made to feel very welcome.

The camaraderie and welcoming nature of the club is one thing that's hardly changed in all my time here. It might be slightly different now because in those early days we didn't sign as many foreign players as we do now. Quite naturally, if I was an English player and I joined a foreign club where there were already English players, I'd be more likely to speak to, and become friends with, them. And that is what happens.

When a young kid joins us, for example take one of Bobby's recent signings Paraguayan Diego Gavilan, there can be a few problems. Of course he needs to learn English and a new way of life, so who better to teach him than fellow South American Nolberto Solano. It's an easier and more relaxed way for him to learn.

We do, however, have someone to look after the players' needs. That person is George Taylor, the club's Player Liaison Officer. He sorts out all manner of stuff for the lads, especially new signings. He gets them insurance, arranges bank accounts, and anything which allows the players to concentrate on settling in and playing football. Kevin started all of this when he began to sign a few foreign players. There is always someone there to help. It's a nice touch and is a real helping hand for the new lads.

What annoys me about some foreign players, though, is that they always think they are technically better than us. And they also think our league is not the greatest. Some of them are over here for the money, that's all, and that is what really annoys me. Despite what they think, I believe technically we're as good as them. Technical ability comes not just from having a great touch, it also comes from the heart and will to battle for the team, it's all mixed into one. I believe that if I went to a foreign country I certainly wouldn't be slagging it off. I would be doing all I could to fit in. But it's like anything, there are a few that think that way and there are others who try and get on with it and mix really well.

Take Philippe Albert who joined us from Anderlecht in Belgium in the summer of 1994. He settled in straight away and loved it here, in fact he became a typical Geordie within months of his arrival on Tyneside. He enjoyed the people, and in return they accepted him with open arms. We also signed Marc Hottiger, the Swiss international during Kev's reign and he was another who settled in immediately.

We made them feel welcome, it was helped because we had such a great team spirit. Even when we signed David Ginola at the start of the 1995/96 Premiership season things didn't change. To be honest, I wasn't so sure when we signed him, he was a Frenchman who was supposed to be quite a moody prima donna. And at first I thought there would be problems. We trained a few times and had a few practice games and the rest of the players seemed to be doing all his running, especially full back John Beresford.

I started having a moan during a training session and after it had finished Keegan pulled me in. He left me in no doubt how he felt. 'Look,' he said, 'I know he's got his faults and I understand what you're saying about his work rate, but he could win us the league! So, if you've got to do a bit extra, then you've got to do it!'

Bez, John Beresford, felt he was being made to look daft at times. It wasn't as if he felt he was doing David's running for him, simply he often had a couple of players running at him without his partner busting a gut to get back and help. Keegan explained to Bez, 'It is one of those things you've got to accept.'

But I've got to admit Ginola's skills were breathtaking. Some games he won for us on his own. And after Keegan explained his point of view I was fine about things. For the first six months Ginola was on fire and did so much to help the cause, some of his play was absolutely blinding.

Some of the touches he would produce before throwing over pin-point crosses for Les Ferdinand were fantastic moments of skill I will never forget. When David Ginola is on fire I don't think there is a more exciting sight in football, but unfortunately it all went sour in the end leaving a bitter taste with our fans – something they have not forgiven him for.

But getting back to those first few months of mine on Tyneside, everything seemed to take off around me, it was unbelievable. And only now, when I look back, do I really take in the significance of what it all meant, to players, the club as a whole and our supporters who had never experienced anything like it.

We were going very, very well almost from the first game of our championship-winning season, in the new Division One, of 1992/93. We were almost always top of the league after an opening run of eleven straight wins, brought to an end by Grimsby Town at St James' Park! Then, with just over three months of the season remaining the manager decided we needed a well earned breather to recharge the batteries in preparation for the final games. We all went out to Marbella. It was a really relaxing break, and we returned refreshed. None of us had any concerns because we were playing extremely well. We would come back and continue to beat all before us … or so we thought.

The first signs of a problem came with a trip to Portsmouth. We got beaten 2–0 and came back to earth with a bump. That was a hell of a shock to us. We didn't even play well, even though I accept Pompey were a good side. A little after that Portsmouth went above us in the table, even though it was only for 12 hours or so. Our stuttering form continued. We had a couple of goalless draws before we travelled to face Tranmere Rovers. At this stage we weren't too bothered by recent results as we had two or three games in hand over our rivals, Pompey. We beat Rovers comfortably 3–0 and I played up front scoring two goals.

We were scared of no-one, in fact the only thing the players feared was the dreaded Terry Mac phone call before games. If you got one of these calls it was to tell you the gaffer wanted a word with you. That meant only one thing, the dreaded 'custard pie.' Custard pie was the term we associated with the news that Keegan was about to tell someone they were dropped. We'd turn up for a game and you could tell immediately by looking around who was out. You would ask, 'Playing?' and they would say, 'No, not today I've had a custard.'

Having steadied the ship with a good win at Tranmere we hammered Brentford and drew with Charlton, both games being played at home. Then Kevin got the cheque book out. He decided to liven things up even more when he signed a young striker called Andy Cole for £1.75 million. As far as the lads were concerned Andy was just some young kid who was playing for Bristol City. But how he was to explode upon the scene in a quite unforgettable style.

I remembered him from when we played against City in early January when we beat them 2–1 at Ashton Gate. Although they lost, Andy had been quite a handful and played extremely well. And from the moment we signed him he had an impact. He made his debut as a sub at Swindon Town, never a favourite ground of the Geordies, coming on for the last 20 minutes or so in a game we lost 2–1.

Then he really started to turn it on. We played Notts County next at home and won 4–0, obviously he scored one. The reaction towards him was great, as soon as he scored the whole team mobbed him. Everyone wanted to see him score, it was so important for Andy to get off to a good start and he did. The Geordies loved him for it. But then they always have loved their number nines.

I didn't know anything about the history connected with the number nine shirt at Newcastle United until I came here, but I soon found out. It's one of those things peculiar to this club, for whoever wears the number nine shirt is expected to wear it well. David Kelly, who was something of a legend on Tyneside wore it with pride and he did very well in it. Signed by Ossie Ardiles in 1991 from Leicester City, Kelly had a great strike-rate, scoring 39 goals in 83 matches, in an 18-month spell at the club.

We had a decent team when I arrived at the club, but Keegan was adding to it all the time, never standing still, and Coley was just another piece to his never ending jigsaw. I have heard Andy described as surly. To be honest he comes over to me like that as well now. But at the time when he came in from the West Country, the only thing he did wrong in our eyes was move to Crook – nothing against Crook, but it is a good 20 miles south of Newcastle city. That made him something of an outcast. I think he became a bit lonely and homesick.

But he was always considered one of the lads and we had some fun moments with him. I remember one time he came into the dressing room wearing a new jacket. It was one of those fancy designs, probably cost him a fortune – it had a load of weird colours all over the back. As soon as he walked in Keegan called for silence and we thought the meeting was about to begin.

'Right,' said Keegan, 'before we start I want to make it clear that I'm not standing for this. Andy's come in with a nice new jacket today and already one of you has taken a spray can to the back of it.' The whole dressing room fell about and I'm sure Andy saw the funny side.

But while he had those lighter moments you could see he had another side of him. It was apparent when Keegan sent him home one time. Andy had scored in a 2–1 defeat at Southampton on 24 October, 1993. We were due to play Wimbledon in the Coca-Cola Cup the following Wednesday, so the squad stayed in the south in between. Because Coley had some family down there and he was feeling a bit homesick I think he asked the manager if he could have a bit of time off to go and see them. But Kevin said he had to stay with the squad.

Obviously Andy reacted and an argument ensued. 'Look, if you want to go then go, you're no use to me here,' Keegan told him, and that was it, he went.

This might have been a hangover from the previous game at Southampton, when there was an incident with Lee Clark – because Clarky and Andy were great friends. It all kicked off literally at The Dell. We were losing as well as playing badly but Lee, in my opinion, was the best of a bad bunch. Keegan obviously didn't agree and he withdrew his number ten.

Clarky was furious and headed straight for the tunnel which was down near the corner flag, rather than taking a place on the bench as is normal when a player is subbed. It caused a bit of a scene because Keegan raced after him, dragged him back and told him to sit down alongside the rest of the subs on a very tight bench. Clarky started effing and blinding at the manager before kicking over a bucket of water. All of this occurred right in front of Sky Television cameras for the whole country to see!

Keegan went crazy and it took some time for Kevin to forgive him. Clarky genuinely thought he might be sold and forced out of the club he loves because of his indiscretions.

But Clarky wasn't the only one to face the wrath of Keegan's tongue! Kevin could certainly dish it out when he needed to. I remember one time we were playing QPR at home and before the game I was jogging around in the dressing room in some new boots which looked quite snazzy with a bright yellow flash on them. I kept asking the gaffer, 'How do they look? How do they look?' – constantly! Anyway, I went out for the first half and managed to have a shocker. Probably the worst performance I've ever given. And the team as a whole were awful as well.

When we came in at half time Keegan was none too pleased. He started having a go at a few of the lads before he turned to me. '…And as for you,' he said 'get those f**king boots off now!' So I chucked them in the corner and put my old ones back on. It didn't make much difference though. I think he pulled me off within a quarter of an hour of the restart anyway!

I am often asked whether I think the team which won us promotion to the Premier League in 1992/93 was better or more exciting than the side we had a couple of years later containing Tino Asprilla, Les Ferdinand and Alan Shearer.

Actually I believe the strongest Newcastle side I have been part of was in 1995 when we signed David Ginola, Warren Barton and Les Ferdinand. I felt then we had a physically stronger team as well. Warren, who had always impressed in the Wimbledon midfield replaced Marc Hottiger, who was a good player, but being straight he wasn't physically strong.

David Ginola really was a great player during those opening months of his time here, and in my time at the club probably the best to have ever worn a Newcastle shirt. He's a big bloke as well, very strong and very difficult to knock off the ball. He goes over a lot, but he is still strong. Les is also very physical and he was a great partner to Al. It's a shame they didn't stay as a partnership, but Les moved on to Spurs. In fact I still think they would be potent even now, a few years on.

We finally reached the promised land at the end of the 1992/93 season, a campaign in which we lost only eight times, including only one defeat at St James' Park at the hands of Grimsby Town. And we certainly finished in style. We went into the Premiership for the first time on the back of an amazing 7–1 defeat of Leicester City on the final day of the season.

However, the boss gave an insight into his amazing will to win, three days before that carnival day. We played Oxford United at our place even though we were officially promoted the Tuesday before when we went to, of all places Grimsby and won 2–0. So the party had already been running for two days when we faced Oxford.

We were terrible, and only drawing 1–1 at half time. You can guess how upset the gaffer was when we walked into the dressing room. He was furious and told us that if we didn't improve he'd go home rather than watch such rubbish! To say he wasn't happy with the way we were playing is the understatement of the year. In the end, we won the game 2–1, but Keegan had already gone.

So high were his standards that he wasn't prepared to see us perform poorly, he knew just what we meant to the supporters and how much money they had spent following us that season. The under-par performance against Oxford really got to him as he felt we had let the fans down.

But how different the mood was on the Sunday afternoon for the arrival of Leicester. There was certainly no Fog on the Tyne that day! Before the final game started, we were awarded the championship trophy, but the real fireworks were kept for the game itself. There was a truly great atmosphere awaiting us as we made our last minute preparations. Keegan said, 'There's a carnival going on out there, but don't make the game into a carnival.' This time we listened.

Leicester did not know what hit them in that first half, we went in at the interval 6–0 up – it was quite fantastic! I remember the chairman Sir John Hall singing, 'We are the champions,' in the new stand which was being rebuilt. While Keegan had been disappointed a few days before, this time he came into the dressing room at the interval, sat down and said, 'I can't say anything now.' He didn't either, he just sat there smiling to himself.

We were now on a major rollercoaster, an unstoppable crusade which the manager and his chairman were determined would end in Premiership glory. The ground was changing almost every week as the board did their best to try and accommodate all the fans who wanted to follow the Pied Piper of football.

However, I think that although we had a very good team, we didn't have much back-up, much strength in depth behind our first team squad. For instance, we didn't have our own training ground after having moved out of the one we owned on the outskirts of the city because it simply wasn't big enough as the club exploded in size and quality. The stadium was only half re-built and, most significantly, after a glut of fine youngsters – Lee

Clark, Steve Watson, Steve Howey, Robbie Elliott and Alan Thompson – we didn't have much else coming through.

We felt on the field we were very close to seriously challenging the crown jewels of the English Premier League – Manchester United. But in other areas of the club we were five or ten years behind.

One of Kevin's hallmarks was his love of training and pushing us hard. He knew that if we were to have a realistic chance of challenging the top teams for honours the squad needed to be in top shape to get us through the long, hard seasons. The problem was that many of the players who joined us found it very tough to adjust to our training. Steve Guppy was a prime example when he came from Wycombe Wanderers at the start of the 1994/95 campaign. When he joined in our training sessions for the first time I think he just thought it was too much, he was overcome with it all. Especially the five-a-sides. We used to play at a tremendous pace. But now Guppy has progressed really well and deservedly he is now one of the top left-sided players in the league. He has also fulfilled his ambition of having played for England, but at the time he couldn't cope with it up here. I wonder if our fans who travelled to Glasgow to see us play in a four-team tournament with Manchester United, Sampdoria and Rangers that season remember his outstanding performances.

Even Warren Barton, when he first joined in training after his £4 million transfer from Wimbledon in the summer of 1995, said for the first two months, 'I never got a kick in training,' until he settled into the pace of things.

Big defenders on our books at the time, great pros such as Darren Peacock also found it tough. 'Peasy' couldn't handle the five-a-sides either. But he knew he couldn't, so he wasn't bothered.

Darren did well for the team, in fact he was probably our only out and out defender in the side. Others such as Steve Howey and Philippe Albert liked to get forward and play, but Darren knew his limitations and always gave consistent performances for the club. The gaffer knew what he would get from him.

Kevin loved nothing more than bringing in more quality to the club. I remember during the summer of 1993, the end of my first season at the club, I was down in London with Anna and my family when KK rang me out of the blue. He said, 'I've bought someone you'll enjoy playing with.' It was Peter Beardsley, a signing which I was very pleased about.

The following summer he signed Belgian international Albert, and Swiss defender Hottiger who had both performed well in the World Cup. I remember watching Philippe score a couple of goals for Belgium, one of which was a fine effort against their deadly rivals Holland.

So we went into that first season in the Premiership believing there was no reason why we could not continue to take the world on. The confidence was at such a level that nothing fazed us. We didn't see why we could not continue our crusade, although we didn't get off to the greatest of starts.

And I remember our first game, at home against Tottenham. Teddy Sheringham scored the only goal for Spurs, but what I remember most was the manager saying to me before the game, 'They have got a 17-year-old kid making his debut at left-back, he's not bad but he can be got at.' His name was Sol Campbell.

I think some players are totally overrated. But Sol is definitely not one of them. I've trained with him when away on England duty and I think he is one of the best there is anywhere. And I would have him in my team any day. He has splendid pace, as he showed in that game at St James', I didn't get past him once. I tried taking him on for pace and he was too quick; I tried him out in the air and he was too big, I tried muscling him out but he was too strong. I intelligently decided to move inside.

Although we lost to Spurs we played okay, we had a couple of good chances and were a bit unlucky, but at no stage did we lose heart. We then played Coventry City away. We played really well there but once again we were unlucky and lost

2–1. Then we went to Manchester United of all places and I seem to believe that we were written off before we even got to Old Trafford. However, we played with a lot of self belief and got a great 1–1 draw.

After that nervy, obviously tentative start, when we dropped as low as 18th, we settled down to the pace of the league and gradually climbed the table, we were fifth at Christmas and finished a brilliant third. The club continued to grow as did the avalanche of compliments.

Gradually, we became aware of people giving us the title of 'The Entertainers.' And the title was something we were very proud and even protective of. We became known as everyone's second favourite team and Newcastle United shirts began popping up all over the world. At the same time I began to get noticed up and down the country, due mainly to a new role I had been given in the side.

This came about when the manager bought Ruel from Norwich City for £2.25 million. I had been playing out on the wing, until Foxy's arrival, so naturally it crossed my mind that there might be some changes in store. I took a bit of a ribbing from the rest of the lads, they were saying I'd be out of the side, because I'd lost the wide role, and that I was finished. They had already packed me off to a London club! Fortunately, I didn't believe this, nor did the lads – they simply singled me out for some good-natured stick. That was the prevalent thing under Keegan, the atmosphere in the dressing room was so good no-one took the hump.

I tend to think, well I now know, that Keegan always knew what he was going to do with me. Of course he moved me inside to the central midfield role, where I have played ever since.

Aside from my personal considerations, the more pressing thing at the time was for the team to continue to settle into the rigours of the step up in class, from Division One to the Premiership where if you make one mistake you are far more likely to be punished. Of course we noticed a big difference between the divisions, the main one being that the players in the Premiership were technically more comfortable and defenders were able to play a lot more, rather than the more physical approach of the lower league. There's a simple explanation – they are just better players. If you made a mistake it was a goal. In the first division you could get away with it a lot more. We knew with our strike force we were always likely to score more than our opponents, but for the Premiership we needed to get a lot tighter defensively.

But we learnt very quickly how to adapt. And it only took us two or three games to become a force. We had Andy Cole up front for starters. Although his partner, David Kelly, had by now left the club, his replacement wasn't bad – it was Peter Beardsley after all.

David, or 'Ned', as we called him did a great job for us and he was loved by everyone. I was very disappointed when he left. He was a really funny man who did a great deal for the club and for team spirit. He knew just what it meant to wear the number nine shirt at Newcastle. Even now I know the fans appreciated his efforts for us and whenever he returns Ned gets a great reception. I got on very well with him off the field and we still speak on the phone now.

So his departure was a big disappointment, but Keegan had his own idea of who he wanted to play up front after we had gained promotion in such exciting style, and I guess Ned didn't fit into those plans.

As the stature of the club and developments of the ground grew rapidly, so the team had to keep pace. The players that we were buying were more and more high profile and the fees were growing in parallel because of this. I think I was especially fortunate to have been already well established at the club while all this was going on. It must have been quite difficult for some of the new players to join at a time of such transition.

Everything was going well, the atmosphere in the camp was brilliant and the relationship between manager and players was excellent.

Naturally there was the occasional upset, even argument, but generally everything was great. Things were ticking along nicely in the league and we were looking forward to a good Cup run. We drew Luton Town at St James' in the third round and laboured to a 1–1 draw. The replay, of course, was down at their place. Goals from a young John Hartson and Paul Telfer knocked us out of the competition 2–0.

After the game we went by coach down to Bournemouth to relax and try to forget about the game. We had a league game at Wimbledon on the Saturday so it wasn't worth travelling back up north. When we got there Keegan said, 'It's just one of those results you cannot help, don't worry about it, go out and have a drink.' Which we did. Then the infamous Venison, Howey, Mathie incident occurred. Those three players went out the following day as well, when the squad were supposed to be winding down at an Indoor Bowling Centre. Basically they went missing. I remember seeing Keegan, he was absolutely fuming. We were playing on the Saturday and this was Thursday by now.

After just being beaten in the FA Cup it is not every manager who would say, 'Go on have drink and forget about it,' and I think Keegan probably wishes he hadn't said it. I think the players concerned would all agree now that they took advantage of his goodwill. They probably regret it now. The funny thing was that when Keegan went looking for them he found them in the first pub around the corner. So they weren't really that clever in terms of what they did and where they went. This incident put a bit of a dampener on things before the Wimbledon game, and we got beaten by them too. I remember Keegan saying to latest signing Fox, 'Hey, if you want to go back son you can. It's not normally like this.'

But we overcame that wobble, the squad quickly united again and by virtue of losing only two league games in our final 14, we finished third. It was a great achievement, and while I thought we'd always finish in the top half even I was pleasantly surprised with our success.

The next season, our second in the Premiership, we continued to grow in confidence. This time we got off to the best possible start. We travelled to Filbert Street to play Leicester City, a game shown live on Sky. We won 3–1 with Andy Cole, Peter Beardsley and Robbie Elliott scoring the goals. We carried the momentum for our first home game of the new season, Coventry City were the unfortunate victims. We stuffed them 4–0 and I got a couple of the goals. Many people who had doubted us in the first season were now fans of ours.

Sadly it didn't last. After a strong start we faded, eventually finishing sixth and, crucially, just

Left: Aged six months, with those footballer's thighs developing nicely.

Below: Standing to attention with my two brothers, Mark, left, and Dean, centre.

Left: Collecting my first major trophy from Keith Coleman of West Ham United.

The Pegasus team, with me in the front row, far right, at the age of 14.

Left: In action as a 16-year-old for Sovereign, not long before I got my big break.

Right: The Hornchurch Youth team, 1981/82. I'm in the front row, second from right.

Left: My first-ever interview for the local *Romford Recorder*, after signing for Charlton in July 1983.

Right: After scoring my first ever hat-trick, for Charlton against Grimsby Town, when pencil ties were all the fashion!

Standing proudly with my dad Reg outside The Valley on a Charlton open day. We both have more grey hair now.

As a flying winger taking on Manchester United's Captain Marvel – keep up Pop!

Cheer up Lennie! We've just won promotion to Division One in the 1985/86 season.

Party time! Travelling back on the Charlton coach from Carlisle after clinching promotion.

Celebrating the *Evening Standard's* Player of the Month award with my joint managers Alan Curbishley and Steve Gritt.

'He comes on and he scores!' The last ever goal at the old Valley, slotted home by yours truly.

Happy Magpie! My first-ever appearance in the famous
black and white shirt of Newcastle United.

Left: No wonder Kevin Keegan and chairman Sir John Hall are smiling – that's probably the best £700,000 they'll ever spend!

Right: Cheering the Geordie faithful with my eldest son Oliver, then aged four.

Below: I always had a great relationship with the Charlton faithful, as they show on my return to The Valley.

I'm back! My return to first-team action at Old Trafford in August 1999 after my exile under Gullit.

The lads letting their hair down … on a team-building exercise in the Toon.

Don't try this at home … our enigmatic but much loved Colombian striker Tino Asprilla showing his usual flamboyance.

Above: Champions! Celebrating our promotion to the Premier League, 1992/93.

Left: Celebrating with one of England's greats, Stuart Pearce, after he scored in the Champions' League against Dinamo Kiev in October 1997.

Time to relax. At a Sportsman's evening with team-mates Warren Barton and Alan Shearer.

missed out on Europe. Many of the fans have their own opinion why our season went downhill – in January 1995 we suffered the loss of Andy Cole, to championship rivals Manchester United.

The build-up to Andy going to United halfway through the 1994/95 campaign was strange – in fact it was a total surprise. None of us throughout the squad had any inkling at all that Kevin was going to produce this huge shock to the whole Geordie nation. I found out about it the same way our fans did, watching the lunchtime news on the telly. I was obviously very disappointed.

It wasn't as if we were playing too badly although I know we were finding goals hard to come by, but after drawing 0–0 at home to Manchester City we were hit with the bombshell. Andy hadn't scored for quite a few games, six it was, but we were all confident he would come back soon enough.

I think in the end after a lot of personal soulsearching, Keegan just thought that maybe the Premiership teams had found us and our centre forward out. Remember, it was Andy who had been scoring the majority of our goals and with him out of sorts it was always going to be much more of a struggle. True enough, myself and Peter Beardsley chipped in with a few goals – by January I had seven league goals and Peter five – but most of our offensive play was built around Andy. But the more I have looked back at the period over the years, I feel

Kevin thought we were becoming too predictable, and easier to stop, especially if Coley wasn't hitting the target. I had the greatest faith in everything Kevin had done in the past so why should I start doubting him now! Whatever he did was good enough for me.

Anyway, as everyone in football knows the deal was completed and Andy Cole, one of the crowd's great favourites, was on his way to Old Trafford for £7.25 million. We got Keith Gillespie the £1 million-valued winger, in part exchange and KK seemed happy with his part of the deal.

However, although Christmas was still sharp in the memory there was little goodwill from the Geordie faithful. They had lost their beloved number nine and KK was forced to explain his actions to a small crowd of Newcastle followers on the main steps of St James' Park.

Once again, Kevin demonstrated what a great man he was and is. He loved those supporters and felt they had the right to vent their feelings to him. Who else would explain himself to the fans in such an honest and upfront fashion? He didn't have to do that, he was the manager after all and the fans knew he must have had good reasons. But, as the newspaper photographers and television cameramen caught on film, he was there, he explained himself. Despite a slow start, Andy has done brilliantly for Alex Ferguson, but his sale was still proven to be the correct decision for the long term future of the club.

Some fans still probably find his departure hard to accept, especially when you consider that we only finished sixth at the end of that season and missed out on Europe. They feel it was the wrong decision to sell him. But Kevin's intention was always to sell Andy and replace him with Les Ferdinand. But QPR wouldn't let Les go until the end of the season.

By this stage Andy was already on his way out. So what was Kevin to do? There was no point him going out and wasting a few million on another striker just as a stop-gap, when he knew he was going to get the man he wanted in six months' time.

Ironically, our next game saw Man United come to St James' Park and the crowd gave the manager a rousing welcome. They were willing to show their support for his decision and how he appreciated it. We drew 1–1 and Coley's replacement, Paul Kitson, scored our equaliser in the second half.

I honestly believe in my heart of hearts that we came back stronger than ever the following season. Of course the loss of Cole affected us badly in the short term and we only finished sixth, but in 1995/96 we were on fire and, as I will discuss later, we should have gone on and won the title. So, in the long term Keegan's decision proved correct in my opinion.

But it will go down as one of Keegan's greatest risks. The decision to sell Cole was obviously an odd one because there were no obvious weaknesses in his game. I always thought he had a great touch, and he had great pace, no doubt. While personally I always thought he was very aware of people around him. Probably the only thing you could say against him was he missed as many opportunities as he scored.

Yet he was still a prolific scorer – he fired a club record tally of 41 goals in only 45 League and Cup games in season 1993/94, taking the proud record of former club heroes Hughie Gallacher and George Robledo.

We created so many chances for him. Some used to fall on his left foot which wasn't his strongest but he would always cleverly try and manoeuvre himself round onto his right side. Then on another occasion he would smash one in with his left foot. Against Chelsea, he smashed an unbelievable goal from miles out as we attacked the Leazes End of the stadium, and that was with his left foot. It went straight into the top corner and none of us hardly blinked. He really was a one-off.

For so much of the time he was at the club – remember he played only 83 games firing an amazing tally of 68 goals – he was on fire. So the day he left, I felt a little of the blues like everyone else. I would consider he got on well with everybody. In fact I would say we never had a single day's problem with him.

It was around this time, and over the subject of Andy Cole's transfer to Manchester United, that I got into a dispute with the editor of the local *Evening Chronicle*. I did an interview for the paper after Andy had left in which I stated that we missed an Andy Cole type of player, a natural goalscorer if you will. But, as journalists often do, they twisted it and produced a big headline quoting me as saying that we shouldn't have sold him. I knew I hadn't said that, and so did they, but the damage was done. Kevin was livid and I asked the *Chronicle* for an apology, which never came.

As a result I refused to speak with them for several years afterwards. I'm quite a stubborn sort of person and I didn't want to have anything to do with them after that, but I do speak to them now. Incidentally, one of their journalists, Alan Oliver, was particularly supportive of the way I was treated by Ruud Gullit, a few years later.

But back to that 1994/95 season and with Andy gone we had to now rely on Paul Kitson who had been signed on for a while. He took the number nine shirt and he did extremely well for us. However, I never thought he got his dues, he was now being forced to play up front on his own which was not ideal for him. He got a bit of a rough time and yet he scored ten goals that season and never lacked bottle when the going became tough.

Obviously, I think he would have much preferred the luxury of playing with Alan Shearer or Les Ferdinand, but neither had arrived by then. Paul was a lovely lad and he was well liked within the dressing room. Although he was a Murton, County Durham, boy he actually supported Newcastle United as a kid so he was very proud to play for his club as well. Paul was a competitive bloke, he loved playing the gaffer at squash before we commenced training.

That was another aspect of training Keegan was very fond of, squash and head tennis. When I first joined Newcastle I'd never played head tennis before, it wasn't something we did at Charlton, but Kevin used to play and he was so competitive too. I remember my first training session, he got me into the gym and said, 'Get yourself a partner and me and Terry Mac will take you on.' I think he gave me Franz Carr.

And they battered us! They both hopped off with their hands over their eyes in mock-shame, crowing about how good they were, something which they always used to do. But gradually, as the years went by, I found out who could *really* play head tennis. Me and John Beresford used to give Kevin and Terry Mac a good game and I think we were the champions until Bez got injured. They got annoyed when we used to beat them, and while they were very good at it, they used to have a moan at each other when they were losing.

We used to have great fun before training, and people would get in early just to play head tennis. Kevin would come in, maybe he'd be a bit late, and although there would be a queue, he'd barge to the front. 'Come on lads, I'm manager,' he'd say. But it was great fun and we all loved training. There was never a day when I didn't enjoy going in.

Keegan's training methods were totally different to anything I'd ever experienced. We never worked on set plays. I can probably count on one hand the corners we took. His attitude was that we were all good players and if we wanted to work on corners then that was fine, but he certainly didn't push us into it.

As I've said, all we really used to do was five-a-sides. And Kevin enjoyed it more than the players! Him and Terry Mac were always right at the centre of things, one of them on each side. They set up the matches with Young v Old, Geordies v The Rest and so on, and some of the Geordies, especially Lee Clark, took it really seriously. But Keegan was the worst. Suddenly you would feel a tug of your shirt and he would be right up behind you. He'd say things like, 'I'm marking you today so watch it!' Give him his due, he used to run his socks off and if he scored he'd be off round the training pitch with his hand in the air celebrating.

It sounds great fun and it was. But you had to take it seriously. You had to have the same attitude as the manager or you wouldn't last the pace. It was always two-touch football and we played at a frantic pace. We got so many injuries because of it as some players found it just too tough.

Another trick of Keegan's which he used to spice up training a bit, and generally create a good spirit, was to introduce a forfeit for saying or doing the wrong thing, whether it was at training, on the team bus, or whatever. If you got your words mixed up or you trod on the ball the penalty was down on the ground for five press-ups. And it wasn't just for the players. Kevin and Terry Mac used to get involved as well.

One incident in particular involving this will go down in Newcastle folklore. We were playing Leeds and losing 1–0, before I managed to score an equaliser. Then right near the end Peter Beardsley put us 2–1 in front. With the clock running down the ball went out of play and the ref blew his whistle to signal a throw. With that, Keegan, who'd clearly got his wires crossed, grabbed the ball and leapt out of the dugout celebrating a famous victory. Warren Barton came jogging over to take the throw. 'What are you doing Gaffer?' he said. 'It's only a throw.' So, quick as a flash Keegan chucks him the ball and gets down on the turf by the touchline and, in front of a packed stadium, starts to do his five press-ups.

You can imagine the scene. All the players fell about. It was lucky there were only a few seconds left. If it had been any longer, Leeds would definitely have equalised, because all our players were too busy laughing.

It happened another time with Scott Sellars. He tried to take a corner and kicked the corner flag by accident. So, down he went, in front of the opposition's fans, to take his punishment. Keegan was full of praise afterwards. 'Good boy, Scott, you did your five there. Well done.'

They were blissfully happy days, the team was playing well, the team spirit was at an all-time high and Keegan was bringing more and more quality players to the club. Things were about to get even better.

CHAPTER FIVE

SO CLOSE

The season 1995/96 will forever be remembered as the one in which Newcastle United threw away the club's first real opportunity to secure the league title in 69 years. And yet, I maintain it was more the fact that Manchester United won it, rather than we lost it!

I accept I am in the minority over this but I feel the facts back up my case. In my opinion it was not down to a friendly Colombian, Faustino Asprilla who we signed in February 1996, as many suggest. He was a brilliant player with no end of skills, and although he had his faults he cannot be solely to blame for our failure to win the championship. Some fans have blamed his unorthodox style of play which changed the balance of the team. It might have been a contributory factor, I don't know, but it wasn't the sole reason.

Instead I put it down more to the brilliance of two great Manchester United stars – the wonderful Gallic influence of Eric Cantona, but even more so to the form of their great Danish goalkeeper Peter Schmeichel. Without these two I am certain even now there would be parties going on somewhere in the city of Newcastle, on the strength of our league championship win. It would have meant so much to the people of this city but sadly it wasn't to be.

Schmeichel was almost unbeatable at times, his agility and ability to cut down the angles to an onrushing forward, thereby making the goal seem a very small target, were outstanding. He had many talents and every one of them caused problems for opposition strikers. His saves kept Man United in a lot of games. We certainly found this to be the case on an emotional evening in late March 1996 when he almost single-handedly held us at bay in front of 36,000 screaming, passion-filled Geordies. We simply pulverised Man U, and Schmeichel in particular, for over an hour. The rest of their side was creaking at the seams but the Great Dane held firm. After we had battered them for so long it broke our hearts, when Cole crossed to the far post for Cantona to fire home almost unopposed. Cruel luck indeed!

If the season's ultimate failure broke the players'

hearts, and clearly affected our early performances the following year, then how must Keegan have felt? He knew just how close we were to becoming known to the people of Tyneside as one of the greatest Newcastle United sides of all time. He would have loved that tag for his group of 'entertainers' – those fans' opinions meant so much to their Messiah.

The simple facts are that while we produced a wonderful run of results until February, Alex Ferguson's men more than matched that run with a staggering sequence of results of their own from Boxing Day onwards. In fact Boxing Day was significant for another reason. This was the day they defeated us 2–0 at Old Trafford, and put the first real dent in our championship ambitions.

At the time of that first meeting between the two outstanding sides in the division no-one was more aware than Keegan that the result of that match would have such a massive bearing on the eventual outcome of the title race. And so it proved. He knew just how important it was for us to get a positive result of some kind at Old Trafford. While most fans point to our home defeat to Cantona's strike in March as the reason we lost out in the championship race, Kevin still believes to this day that if we had taken just a point at Old Trafford, then we would have been crowned champions! Looking back I don't think any of us realised the moment had been lost, a moment when success would have given us one hand on the title.

A win that evening would have demoralised even Fergie's wonder men, of that I remain sure. Perhaps then, Tino Asprilla, who at this stage was still many hundreds of miles away playing his football in Serie A, would not have had to carry the can for our eventual demise. A victory would have meant we would have gone into the New Year holding an almost unassailable 13-point lead over the men who were eventually to be secured as champions on the final day of the season. Surely, even a great side like that Manchester United team would not have gone on a remarkable run of 15 wins in their remaining 19 games!

Naturally, every game brought us different challenges, but it took until the very end of the year, and those two so hurtful goals from Andy Cole and Roy Keane, before we suffered our third League defeat of the campaign. During the game Keith Gillespie was the victim of a bad challenge by Gary Neville, which put Keith out for the rest of the season, but we didn't even get a free kick! I know a lot of fans say that was a crucial blow because we lost the balance that Gillespie and Ginola had given us. Sure, that was partly to blame, but I don't think it was a major factor.

I know people say the whole country were behind us, but that didn't matter, the game at Man

United was a private battle between two passionate areas of the country. We were, if the media was to be believed, everyone's second favourite side, but unfortunately we found out that finishing second hardly means a thing, no-one remembers the also rans.

A two-line mention in the following season's *Rothman's Football Yearbook* was all we warranted after our dream, and that of our wonderfully inspiring chairman Sir John Hall, KK and many, many thousands of Geordies all over the world, blew up so painfully in our faces.

It was without a shadow of doubt the best Newcastle United side I have been part of, it was a time and team of wonderful flowing football, and also exhilarating exhibitions in front of packed houses, both home and away, all seemingly happy to acknowledge the quality of our attacking play. Great days all! We led the way for so long under the brilliantly buoyant and so brave steerage of Keegan and his always cheery number two Terry McDermott – what a team they were too, that must not be forgotten.

Those times under Keegan were some of the best I've ever experienced and all the players got on brilliantly. Ever since I've been at the club we've had a tremendous team spirit which we've continued away from the football pitch. We have an appointed entertainments manager – it used to be John

Beresford, nowadays it's Warren Barton – and they are responsible for organising nights out to help the players bond. Not that we needed much help!

We always try to organise these nights as often as possible. Some of the regular haunts were Uno's restaurant and Julie's nightclub. It used to be a running joke among the fans that if you didn't see a few of the players in there, something must be up! The best dos were always those at Christmas. It used to be a rule that we had to have a theme. One year, I think it was Christmas 1996, the theme was fancy dress. I turned up as Roy 'Chubby' Brown, Alan went as Terry Mac, wearing a Newcastle shirt and a stupid fake moustache. Everyone joined in from the young players to the foreign lads.

One of the lads took a picture of us before we set off round the town. We had everyone from Spiderman to Cinderella's Ugly Sisters. We must have looked a right sight – all these nutters wandering round Newcastle city centre. We took a ball with us so we could play keep-ups on the way round between pubs. It was mental. I seem to remember we all descended on a shoe shop at one point, half the players started trying on shoes. And all the fans we saw on the way round were cheering us on. They loved it, seeing all their heroes dressed up like idiots.

Another year the theme was bad dress sense so everyone turned up with slicked back hair,

National Health glasses and granddad trousers pulled up to our armpits. Another time we hired a boat and sailed down the Tyne.

We were always ones for dressing up, though. Last Christmas for the official club do, where the players get to take along their wives and girlfriends, me, Alan, Anna and Lainya went as Abba. The girls made the outfits and we really looked the part with our stick-on beards – me and Alan, that is! We had to get up and sing an Abba number as well. Steve Howey, Bez and their wives, together with a blow-up doll came as the Spice Girls and then there was Stuart Pearce. He came as a Mummy and turned up wrapped head-to-toe in bandages!

But whatever the players did, it was always good-natured. No-one ever got into any trouble. When Keegan was here, he used to pretend he had received complaints about us. He had this filing cabinet in his office and he made out it was full of stuff about the players and reports of the things we got up to. 'I'm compiling dossiers on you lot,' he'd say. 'I know what you get up to. I had another complaint last night.' But he was only messing about, there was never too much trouble as far as I was aware.

But back to the start of 1995 and the season where we came so close to pipping Manchester United to the title. Although the season was to end in such deep rooted disappointment, it began with a splash of champagne and so much excitement within the clubs and pubs of Tyneside. In the close season Kevin had got the cheque book out again and new signings Les Ferdinand, David Ginola and Warren Barton, not to mention goalkeeper Shaka Hislop – the lesser known of the quartet but still a big signing – all joined the Toon march and played in an opening day 3–0 hammering of Coventry City.

Everyone was so high on that bright, glorious summer's afternoon, no-one more so than big Les, even though he had to wait until well into the second half before his great moment of glory arrived. Earlier goals from me and 'Pedro' Beardsley had already made the eventual outcome more than secure. However, when the big number nine broke free from just over the half way line to first of all beat a despairing John Filan the Sky Blues keeper to the ball, we all held our breath. Keegan once described his first goal for the club, 13 years earlier, as having been sucked into the net by the crowd, and it was as if that moment had arrived again.

But we need not have worried and the crowd could have saved their breath, because Les buried the ball extravagantly into the far corner from what seemed like at least 35 yards. Both the players and the crowd knew in that moment that a new hero, a new number nine for them to hang their hopes on, had arrived.

The players all knew the significance of the former QPR star's effort. As players like Jon Dahl Tomasson have since found, it is all important to score on your debut especially when, as a big-money striker, you arrive in front of the adoring hordes at St James' Park. We all, nearly to a man, ran and jumped on Les' back in celebration as he seemed set on celebrating with the massed ranks of the main stand crowd. It probably would not be allowed these days!

Unlike the previous season when we got off to a great start, this time we kept it going. We embarked on a run right through to early December, 3 December to be exact, when we lost to Chelsea at Stamford Bridge. During that spell our only other defeat had come at The Dell against Southampton, in early September. Looking back it wasn't much of a surprise because The Dell is something of a bogey ground for us. We have always had trouble getting anything there. Northern Ireland midfielder Jim Magilton scored the only goal for Dave Merrington's men.

But the second defeat to Chelsea was more significant. By now things were beginning to catch up with a few of us. We were starting to pick up a few injuries and certain key players began to go off the boil. I include both myself and Les in this, neither of us managed to match the heights of earlier in the season; while Ginola and Keith

Gillespie, our two previously inspired wingers, were no longer able to produce the quality of crosses as consistently as before.

But it must also be remembered that we were troubled by injuries to any number of players around that time. Both Keith and David missed games as did Steve Howey, who at the time was, in my opinion and that of the England coach, Terry Venables, playing some of the best football of his career.

Despite these setbacks we somehow managed to paper over the cracks, even after our Boxing Day defeat at Old Trafford. We responded in the best way possible – we went on a run of five straight wins, the last of which, against Middlesbrough at The Riverside on 10 February, was the first appearance of Kevin's new Colombian international, Asprilla.

There had been many weeks of on-off speculation surrounding Tino's future in Italy, until then he was playing his wonderful off the cuff brand of football for Parma. But finally Keegan splashed another £7.5 million on the South American star. And what an early impression he made! As I recall he flew in that day to complete the deal. He had hardly been in the country a few hours when he made an unexpected debut appearing as a second half substitute. At the time we were in deep trouble, trailing 1–0 to an own goal from my then roommate John Beresford.

As all Newcastle fans will remember he came on wearing gloves and many people wondered what to make of him. But it didn't take us long to realise we had a real star on our hands. Quick as a flash he began to turn on his magic and within what seemed like minutes we went from 1–0 down to 2–1 up. The finishes from both Steve Watson and Les were not spectacular in their own right, but the build-up from the Colombian with the elastic legs certainly was – those moments of magic will live with me and those 30,000 fans until the day we die.

He turned defenders one way and then the other to produce crosses which simply begged to be put away. We all celebrated afterwards, yet again KK had unearthed a winner.

But as time went on we realised there was another side to Tino. He had a talent which lit up many of our matches but he also had a tendency to become a loose cannon getting in the way of his attacking team-mates such as Beardsley and Ferdinand.

Controversy soon followed for the likeable Colombian. Exactly 14 days after his debut he was reported to the FA after it was alleged he head-butted Manchester City captain Keith Curle, after he had helped us score three equalisers in a pulsating match to gain a 3–3 draw.

As Tino pressed the self-destruct button so our results suffered on the pitch. It was during this period that we lost four in six games as it began to dawn on everyone that Manchester United were going to take our title away from us. We simply couldn't believe the number of times they would score late winners or Schmeichel and Cantona would pick up rave reviews for their part in the victories that continued to come week after week.

It was not until late March, after we suffered a 2–0 defeat at Highbury, that Man United finally overtook us at the top of the table. It was heartbreaking. To go eight out of nine and a half months on top of the table only to finish second is indescribable.

And yet, our actual finish to the season was not as bad as probably some people remember. We only lost two of our final eight matches, at Liverpool and Blackburn Rovers, but how crucial and how cruel those two particular defeats proved in the end. We led both games with minutes remaining, but by the final whistle we'd lost both. The tears of our supporters who finally realised the dream was over and the famous shots of KK hanging over the advertising board which surrounds Anfield, are all that we have to remember from two epic encounters.

Of course, the Liverpool game was a classic. We lost 4–3 in what everyone seems to think was possibly the best and most entertaining Premiership game of all time. We went into the match at Anfield, on 3 April still believing the miracle might happen. It was a never to be forgotten night when the ball seemingly bounced from one net to the other. You simply had no time to take a breather, no wonder Sky Sports' Andy Gray still talks about the match to this day.

Robbie Fowler and Stan Collymore scored a couple each while our goals came from Ferdinand, Ginola and that man Asprilla. I don't have nightmares but if I was to start then I am certain the sight of Stan pulling his leg back before exploding an unstoppable effort past Pavel Srnicek would be a likely candidate for starters. It was little consolation to us at the time that so many people were praising us for our football that night. It didn't mean a thing, we had lost, that was all that mattered.

It was the same story after the defeat by Rovers five days later. Although the odds were going more and more against us we went to Ewood Park still determined to chase Man United all the way.

We lost again, ironically to a goal from a Geordie striker named Graham Fenton. He broke his home town's heart with a last-minute winner after he had minutes earlier equalised a rare David Batty strike. A kid who began his football at the same boys' football club as Alan Shearer dared to end our dwindling hopes of the title. No wonder Fenton has had a few nervy experiences back in his native north-east since! It wasn't his fault – it was simply that errors at the back had began to creep into our game. It was so disappointing because for most of the season we had a remarkably good record in that department – amazing when you look at the attacking formations we put out.

The lads were devastated, it was one of the quietest coach rides back to the north- east I can remember. We knew then that it simply wasn't going to be our year.

However, we were nothing if not determined and after three more wins on the trot we still had an outside chance. Then Keith Gillespie headed home a rare goal for us at Elland Road which enabled us to edge past Leeds. It was all too much for Keegan, the pent up frustration of recent weeks came out in a bitter attack on Man United boss, Alex Ferguson. KK allowed his passion for our football club and his players to explode – and it was caught for posterity by Sky Sports.

The cause for this attack could be traced back a few days earlier when Ferguson dared to hint that Leeds would not try as hard against us as they had in their narrow defeat by Manchester United. Keegan was also angry over suggestions that other sides would treat us in a more laid-back way than they would his side. And in the post-match interview it boiled over. 'I tell you what,' Keegan said, 'I'd love it, I'd really love it if we beat them.'

The media believed Kevin had snapped, and that I am sure was what Alex wanted everyone to think. But he had said things all season, that is just the way he is, he wears his heart very much on his sleeve. We were delighted and fully behind the gaffer's reaction – we knew he was still in control but at the same time we appreciated his passionate defence. We had no idea he was going to blow his top, but afterwards when he got onto the coach he was still fuming. The players weren't impressed by Ferguson's comments! We felt the same amount of anger as our manager in what we thought was an insult to our professionalism, and the other teams in the league.

For the next game we went to Nottingham Forest, our penultimate match of the season. Peter put us in front and we were cruising, until our jinx hit us again. We came up against our bogey man Ian Woan – for some reason he would keep some of his best performances and goals for us, very much as Matt Le Tissier seemed to do when we faced Southampton. Anyway, he cracked one into the bloody top corner out of nowhere – I am sure he was trying to hit the ball up into the stand! That was a massive body blow considering we'd had countless chances to make the game safe. But we never got that added security and we only had ourselves to blame.

Incidentally, we were due to play against Forest a

couple of weeks later in Stuart Pearce's testimonial, but this did not seem to make them any more receptive to our cause. Mind you, nor should it have!

Despite our best efforts and quite a few wins in the final stage of the season, bad results against Liverpool, Blackburn and now Forest had cost us dear. Ferguson's boys were winning week-in week-out. We were left knowing that we had to beat Spurs on the final day of the season and Manchester United had to lose at Middlesbrough. That was never on. Man U took control early on while we struggled to a draw. We had ran out hopeful, but we were not expecting too much because we knew just how well Man United were playing.

Many critics will say that we were eventually victims of Keegan's all-out attacking style. But I would say to that: why worry like the rest of the teams about defending when we had so many offensive-minded players who could go forward, crucify opponents and on many occasions score almost at will? To be fair, that's what we did until a certain Mr Schmeichel came to Toon!

But we should have won it and, but for a couple of slip-ups, we would have. It's as simple as that. I realise now, several years later, what a chance we had to do something very special for the club and the fans. We were not in any way happy to have finished runners-up, that means nothing. As Alan Shearer often says, only winners count.

We were devastated, but we did believe we would come back and win it the following season – but the chance had gone. We talked amongst ourselves after the season and resolved to come back and give Man United a run for their money, and this time not make stupid mistakes. We even signed Alan Shearer from Blackburn for £15 million in the close season, but even he couldn't help us. We just needed to improve in a few areas – it all seemed so simple on paper, unfortunately we play on grass!

So, why did we fail when we were so far ahead before Christmas? I think it was a combination of things, Man United's brilliance, undoubtedly, Tino's erratic behaviour and the fact that two or three of us went off the boil. But it was not pressure, that's for sure. We had players with experience, people like Peter who had won the title before, we had players who had performed in World Cups and other players who'd won things. In the final analysis we just didn't play well enough in the second half of the season.

It is true to say the whole country seemed disappointed for us, it had all stemmed from the year before when they began to like our style and the momentum of our play.

Our biggest regret is that with the personnel we had we should have won it. Our form of defence was attack, with us launching attack after attack then the opposition could hardly get at us. Of course, we ran into problems when we lost possession.

That was, and is, Keegan's style. It is no secret that he liked to sign ball players. Albert was the best ball playing defender I had ever seen, no-one will ever forget him chipping Schmeichel for our fifth goal in the morale-boosting victory over Man United at St James' the following season. And Warren Barton would be the first to admit he is better attacking than defending, it was the same with John Beresford. So, sometimes Darren Peacock was our only recognised defensive minded player in the side. Perhaps that was our undoing.

Keegan believed wholeheartedly in attack, rather than worrying about the defensive side of our game. But I will never blame him for producing some of the most exciting times in the club's long and illustrious history. We may have lost a battle but we came out with our honour intact.

CHAPTER SIX

OUT OF LUCK

When Kevin Keegan's Newcastle United qualified for European competition in 1994/95, after an absence of 17 seasons, we were all very excited. European competition has always been something special. But little did I know that we would start back with such a bang. It was my third full season at St James' Park and after finishing in third position the previous season, our first in the Premiership, we had qualified for the UEFA Cup.

When the draw was made in Switzerland we were pitted against Belgian outfit, Royal Antwerp, with the first leg to be played on the continent. It was a great opportunity for us to judge ourselves against some of Europe's top clubs such as Juventus and Parma, but first we had to get past a side with a fair reputation.

However, in those days we feared no-one and I remember going into the first round-tie over there with us going brilliantly in the Premier League. In truth we were battering everybody as we led the league until early November. Europe was a great challenge, a break out into the unknown, and I sensed even Keegan was a little bit apprehensive about going over to Belgium.

Maybe I should call it a mixture of apprehension and excitement, it was a bit of both. Clearly Kevin was used to the old Liverpool ways when they ruled Europe. But even Liverpool, in their great era of European domination, rarely put on a show to match the one we did in that amazing first leg.

We just went over there and played as if we were playing in the league and our travelling Toon Army loved it. There was no trouble and our supporters seemed to have a great time over there – it was all new to most of them, many of them weren't old enough to remember the last campaign back in the late seventies.

We were on a fantastic high, playing so well anyway, and scoring lots of goals, many of them by me. I started the league season scoring goals for fun, having been moved inside following the arrival of Ruel Fox. It was Kevin's idea to play me inside breaking into the box when the ball was crossed in from the wings. And it worked a treat. I just had the knack of arriving at the right time. I was even outscoring Andy Cole which was no mean feat! Barry Venison was in the holding position alongside me, having himself been switched from right back.

It was around this time, when I was ahead of Andy in the goalscoring charts, that Keegan concluded a post-match interview with Sky Sports by doing an impression of me. It was hilarious and I think perfectly illustrated the sort of rapport I had built up with the manager. Keegan was taking the piss by putting on, what he thought, was a cockney accent. 'I'm so grateful to the gaffer for this chance,' he said. 'It's great to be scoring more goals than Andy Cole. I just hope I can keep it going.' He went on like this for about a minute and I have to admit it was really funny, even though his 'cockney' accent was shocking. And Sky loved it. They kept repeating it for about a week afterwards.

We decided to treat the Antwerp tie like any other and play our usual game. We couldn't have made a better start. Our first tie in Europe in 17 years started with a bang, the ball broke to John Beresford on the left and, when he swung over the cross, I arrived late into the box, threw myself at the ball and my header flew into the net off the inside of the far post – what a start!

Eight minutes later we won the ball again, I played it out wide to Foxy, he broke down the wing and then put over an inch perfect cross between

Andy and myself. I got there first and, with another header, buried it into the roof of the Antwerp net. Unbelievable! I completed my hat-trick of headers six minutes after the break to put us four up. Marc Hottiger, our right back, crossed once again from that flank for me to guide it low into the bottom corner. Absolutely unbelievable!

I've scored a few headers before, one against Chelsea in the 2000 FA Cup semi-final. But I've never scored three in a game like that. Mind you, even scoring a hat-trick of headers doesn't come close to the wonder goal I 'scored' in March 1993. It was during the promotion year and we were playing Brentford at home. During the game, the Brentford keeper cleared the ball and it fell to me standing about 20 yards inside our own half. As it came down I volleyed it straight back over the keeper's head. It would have been one of the best goals ever, certainly better, and further out, than the wonder goal David Beckham scored against Wimbledon a few seasons ago. The only problem was Barry Venison appealed for offside against one of the Brentford players just as their keeper cleared it and the ref blew up. I think we were winning 5–1 at the time so it didn't make much difference to the result, but I'm not sure Keegan would have been too pleased if it had been 0–0 at the time.

But having said that the hat-trick I scored against Antwerp was a really big moment. After the game I was being interviewed on the pitch by a BBC television crew. They were asking me a few questions when Keegan came up behind me and planted a big kiss on my cheek. 'This lad is good enough to play for England,' he said. At that moment I had never been selected for my country so it was well timed. I remember speaking to Bez in the airport before we flew home and he said, 'Your profile is going to go through the roof after this!' And to be fair he was spot on – my England call came not long after.

With the ability of team-mates such as Peter Beardsley (who was returning to the team for the first time after a face injury), Scott Sellars and Ruel Fox, we were devastating that night and in the end it could well have finished up in a cricket score.

That summer we had signed Peter for £1.3 million. And while he was the success we all knew he'd be, his second spell at Newcastle didn't get off to the greatest of starts. One of his first games was a match at Anfield to play in Ronnie Whelan's Testimonial. It was a full house and Liverpool were unveiling their new signing from Spurs, Neil Ruddock. It was his first game at Anfield and while he might not have gone out to try and impress everyone, he was certainly treating it as a real game and putting himself about a bit.

Anyway, after hitting Lee Clark with a tough challenge early on, in the second half he went up with Peter. Pedro got an arm in the face and he collapsed in a heap. Keegan was furious. I don't know if Ruddock did it intentionally or not but he was certainly hyped up for the game. We lost Peter for quite a few weeks.

I have seen the clash countless times on television since and cannot make up my mind. Ruddock certainly wasn't looking at Peter when he did it so perhaps it wasn't intentional. He was just out to impress the Kop and make himself a favourite, and to be fair he did!

But it was a major disappointment for us, and Peter, because we were all looking forward to playing with him. He didn't return to action until that UEFA Cup tie in Antwerp. By rights Peter still wasn't 100 per cent and he should have worn some sort of face-protection, like the mask made famous by Gazza, but Peter didn't fancy wearing anything like that. Kevin was so desperate to have him back that he played him out on the wing in Belgium and told him to keep out of trouble. It was important to the team to bring him back, the unfortunate thing was that he had to leave Steve Watson out for him and Steve had started the season on fire, and had been scoring a right few goals. He was unlucky to be left out, but the result justified the change. Mind you Steve did come on as a sub late on and scored our fifth goal.

But Peter's troubles weren't over. Incredibly,

exactly the same thing happened to him on the first day of the following season – a televised Premiership game away at Leicester City. The game was already over as a contest, with us comfortably ahead when Peter got caught with another flying arm. Down he went in a heap, and we lost him for another six-eight weeks. It was a terrible disappointment, but at least Peter could laugh about it. He said it didn't affect his looks!

The thing about Beardsley was that he made it so much easier for the rest of us, because he was so talented and unselfish. His style of play left so many gaps because centre halves didn't know whether to come out and pick him up playing in the hole. If they did, it left a gap at the back for me to exploit, allowing me to break through into the space beyond our strikers. Beardsley was the best, and a pleasure to play with.

We were really attacking with purpose at this time. It suited the manager and it suited Coley as well. Remember, we had Scott Sellars on one wing and Foxy on the other. Ruel was an out and out winger, he'd stick out there on the touchline causing problems for the opposition, while Scott used to come inside more and either shoot or set us up with quality passes. We were so well balanced, with Barry Venison, 'Venners', just sitting in behind me. He was the insurance for me to increasingly get into the opposition box. And against Antwerp I managed to put the chances away.

After the tie in Belgium, we won the return leg 5–2. Inevitably, I scored the first. It gave us a 10–2 aggregate win. All these goals were doing me no harm at all. I really felt I was beginning to get noticed, not just in Newcastle but also in London, and it was great.

I really enjoyed my first taste of European football and couldn't wait for the next round. The trouble was we started to develop a bit of a jinx regarding injuries.

In all the time I've been at Newcastle, we have had a very good first team, and maybe one or two others could come in and do well. But we have always had small squads and whenever we've picked up injuries we have struggled, especially up front.

This always seemed to be the case in European games. There is no way Man United would use Roy Keane or Gary Neville as a striker, is there? But Keith Gillespie, our right winger and Steve Watson, a full back, played up front for us. We certainly didn't have the strength in depth that we needed to compete in the major competitions. Most of it I consider to be bad luck. If our forwards hadn't all got injured at the same time we wouldn't have had to play people out of position.

You need a certain amount of luck and especially that the spine of your team don't get injured.

People often suggest the club is jinxed, sometimes I wonder! We've been so close to winning the league, the FA Cup and tasting success in Europe. We've been so near and yet so far away to winning a trophy at this club. That has got to be my number one aim before I hang up my boots, to reward the fans with a trophy.

A group of us were sat in the dressing room recently and started to discuss our problem with injuries. Alan Shearer is a classic case. He admitted to having had 12 operations. And even the young Carl Serrant, who is only 24, has had eight. It's ridiculous. Our Welsh international skipper, Gary Speed admitted to having had only two operations, although one of those was for a varicose vein so that doesn't count. I count myself very lucky, maybe it's because we tough midfielders aren't as soft as the rest!

It was another case of what might have been that first season back in Europe. After thrashing Antwerp we lost in the second round to Atletico Bilbao, on away goals. I was injured for the first leg at St James', but the lads were well on their way to winning the tie. We were cruising at 3–0 up, but then we lost our concentration. The crowd started a Mexican wave and unfortunately this seemed to transmit itself to the pitch and the performance clearly dipped. We gave away two silly goals in the final 19 minutes and in the end that cost us a place in the next round.

I will never forget the atmosphere in Bilbao for the return leg – it was so special, just ask our fans. Before we went out there everyone kept going on about the hostility we could expect and how the Spanish were going to be towards us. But we never experienced any of it. Naturally, we got the boos when we went on to the pitch, but that's to be expected. Otherwise the atmosphere was magnificent – a great advert for European football.

Neither Coley, nor another of our strikers, Alex Mathie, were fit so we started with Steve Watson, our right back up front on his own. Steve is a very versatile player but he'd admit himself he is no striker. I was told by Keegan to get forward as much as I could to support Steve, and it so nearly paid dividends. In the first half, I had a great chance and it was odds on that I would score. I made a run past Steve and Peter threaded a great ball straight over the defenders' heads. I thought I'd control it with my left foot, and then fire it home with my right into the corner. But it hit my foot and bounced off like a trampoline, straight into the keeper's arms.

It was a great chance and, given the form I was in, I would have expected myself to have scored. I've done it hundreds of times in games, in training, but this time it let me down. People don't need to remind me about that miss, it is something I will never forget. I should have scored and then Bilbao would have needed to score twice to knock us out. Our confidence was such that I am certain we would have gone on and had a good run in the competition. But that was it, we were out of Europe.

This wasn't to be the only time we were unlucky in Europe. I remember Monaco, home and away, Barcelona away, and PSV home and away when we had six or seven international players, including me, sitting on the bench all injured; and even in Belgrade when I went down ill on the day of the game – these were all examples of us paying dearly for a mixture of bad luck and lack of a big enough squad to see us through.

It seemed a knack of Newcastle United to suffer from these problems at crucial times. It is not that our physios and doctors aren't professional enough – there is no doubt at all that they are superb. And it always was an affliction affecting our strikers. Coley had major problems with his shin splints which saw him out missing important games for us when he was at his very best.

Despite the injuries we had a great run in the UEFA Cup two seasons later in 1996/97 during which we defeated Halmstads, Ferencvaros, and a strong Metz side which included a certain Robert Pires on the wing. Possibly the best performance was a 3–2 defeat in Budapest, Hungary against Ferencvaros. Although we lost, it was a solid display and for large periods of the game we silenced a very hostile crowd.

Then they came for the second leg and we beat them 4–0 and they didn't know what had hit them. I remember David Ginola scoring a quite unbelievable goal at the Gallowgate End of St James'. I was right behind him screaming at him to leave the ball. But he flicked it up over someone's head with his right foot and then, as it came down, he volleyed it in with his left, high into the top corner. My first thought was, 'Thank God he didn't leave it for me.' I would probably have blasted it high into the stand!

We also played Metz, from Northern France, which was a tough game, even a dirty game at times. I remember Dave Batty got smacked and was left with a head wound by their Brazilian midfielder. There were tackles flying in all over the place. Peter put us in front with a penalty before they equalised late on.

In the second leg Tino was on fire, he produced some tricks only he can produce. He was in absolutely frightening form and he scored an unbelievable goal. His first goal was a penalty, and then he picked the ball up just inside their half, waltzed past three or four defenders and slipped it past the keeper. But when he ran off on one of his celebrations he took his shirt off and waved it in the air with the use of the corner flag. He got a yellow card for his trouble and because of that we lost him for the quarter final against Monaco. I find it strange that you can get in trouble for celebrating a goal, I believe it is part and parcel of football and helps bond the supporters and the players. Fans love to see that it means something to the players when their side scores. Tino's celebrations were something else anyway, he always did somersaults, so twirling round his shirt wasn't that outrageous.

By the time of the Monaco game Kenny Dalglish had replaced Kevin, who had left the club in January, but to be fair our form hadn't dipped under KD. We continued to go into all of our games with huge expectations. Because of Tino's absence yours truly had to go up front. I believe our best side would have beaten Monaco even though their side was littered with internationals. They had Emmanuel Petit playing in midfield, Thierry Henry (now at Arsenal) in their attack, Franck Dumas in the centre of defence along with Giles Grimandi (now also at Highbury) and, last but not least, goalkeeper Fabien Barthez before he signed for Manchester United. Everton's John Collins was in the side as well! But they still only beat us 1–0 at home, and I still believe that if we'd had our full team out we would have taken care of them.

Of course, the return leg in Monaco was always going to be a struggle. We tried our best but they were clearly the better side and thumped us 3–0, making it 4–0 on aggregate. We had great support out there but once again we had to play an emergency striker, Steve Watson once again. Although returning to the region in which he has his home base, David, like many of us, was out of sorts that night. He was at that stage in his Newcastle career when he was either brilliant or a hindrance to us. Maybe the fact that Kevin had denied him a move to Barcelona in the summer was the cause of his inconsistency. I can't be sure but he definitely went off the boil after that.

The Champions League campaign of 1997/98, after we had finished second in the league the previous season, promised so much, surely our jinx could not strike us once again. How wrong could I be. Les Ferdinand was sold to Tottenham that summer and within hours Alan Shearer was out for eight months with a bad ankle injury sustained in pre-season.

We had to pre-qualify. We played Croatia Zagreb over two legs. Without Shearer or Ferdinand we had to rely on our balding Georgian international, Temuri Ketsbaia to score a crucial goal. He fired an extra time winner in Zagreb during the second leg to guarantee our place. This was one of our greatest away performances, one in which we did carry the luck for a change. Croatia Zagreb had any number of full internationals in their side and to go there, in front of an amazingly hostile crowd, and qualify for the Champions League in the Croatian capital was a magnificent result for us and then boss Kenny Dalglish.

The first group game was a remarkable occasion, surely one of the greatest nights in the club's history. Barcelona at St James' was a magnificent five-goal thriller. The brilliant Asprilla was at his wonderfully exciting best, there was the atmosphere of a stadium simply bouncing with the excitement of the whole event and a winger, Keith Gillespie, who turned in possibly his most outstanding performance for the club.

I was later told that Sir John Hall, who had dreamt of this night for years, couldn't even bear to watch the match – he was sat at the back of his box, a nervous wreck! Mind you he would have still known when to celebrate our goals, what a noise that was!

Barcelona are the best known club in the world. I think they and their Dutch coach Louis van Gaal arrived on Tyneside expecting to beat us quite comfortably. And I suppose they had plenty of reason to fancy themselves. No Shearer, no Ferdinand. But they didn't account for our South American jack in the box. Tino, playing up front on his own, got three goals in the opening 50 minutes and we played them off the pitch. They didn't know how to handle us during that spell. Their full back Sergi got probably the biggest roasting he'll ever get in his life from Keith Gillespie.

Then there was De la Pena, who lost his rag and was fortunate to get away with only a booking, when he clattered me shortly after Tino had headed his second of the opening half. The game was being played out in a constant downpour and I don't think De la Pena liked it much – he was more used to the Catalan sunshine.

As a team we played so very well, sticking to the tactics, until they came back at us late on. We started to relax thinking we had got it sewn up, but then they made one substitution, bringing on Christophe Dugarry, and 20 minutes later it was 3–2. They gave us the shock of our lives! In the end we were hanging on for the win – which was ridiculous really. The moment French World Cup star Dugarry came on the game changed. He had a hand in both goals and should have equalised late on. What a travesty that would have been!

We started really well in our group games and after our first away trip, to the Ukraine, people were beginning to fancy us for a place in the quarter finals. We went to Kiev not knowing what we were in for, although we knew Dinamo had a couple of outstanding forwards, Andrii Shevchenko and Sergei Rebrov, and a fanatical crowd backing them. I have never known anything like it, there were 100,000 people there in this massive stadium.

John Beresford had an unbelievable night, he scored two goals and we got a very creditable 2–2 draw on one of the coldest nights I have ever played football. I think it was minus nine. The only down side for me personally was that I went off at half time injured! We were two down by then, so in hindsight it was probably a good decision by the manager!

I had been struggling with a groin injury for a couple of weeks before the tie and I don't think the cold weather did me any favours. I managed to start the game but I probably shouldn't have played. I didn't know it at that time, but that injury cost me a place in England's last World Cup qualifying game against Italy in Rome which will forever be a major disappointment to me.

We were in buoyant mood after our victory over Barcelona and draw in Kiev, but then it all went wrong against the third team in our group, PSV Eindhoven of Holland. We faced PSV with an injury wrecked side. We knew our injury problems, certainly in attack, would catch up with us. I suppose you could say, with plenty of reason, that the two games against PSV on paper should have been the easiest of the group matches. But we soon realised they were no mugs. If you look at their team, they had Jaap Stam, now at Man United, Luc Nillis, who played in Euro 2000 for Belgium and is now at Aston Villa, and they also had Vim Yonk who is at Sheffield Wednesday.

We went there with Ian Rush, who had signed until the end of the season, as our only attacker. All credit to Rushy, he worked his socks off as he manfully tried to create something against a strong home side, but because of injuries we were forced, yet again, to play without our first choice strikers. We lost narrowly, 1–0 despite fielding a much-weakened side. It left us so frustrated, I promise you!

Things were even more farcical for the home leg. I remember looking across the dugout, Dave Batty and I were out suspended and Stuart Pearce, Alan Shearer and Tino were all out injured. Again we lost by a narrow margin with at least six, maybe seven, players sitting next to me on the bench who would have been playing if fit. To this day, I believe we would have qualified for the latter stages if we'd had anything like a full team available. True, Yonk got a great goal in the first leg but we could have beaten them over the two group games, no question.

We seemed at that time to have a terrible record for serious injuries – it was as if the club was being punished.

The following season we qualified for the Cup Winners' Cup and got a terrible draw, a tie against Yugoslavia's top side Partizan Belgrade. But it got worse. At the time NATO was planning an aerial offensive and then, on the day we flew out there, there was an earthquake which registered seven on the Richter scale. As if the atmosphere wasn't unfriendly enough!

Unfortunately, I picked up a bug and missed the game. But we fought hard and but for Batts giving away a dubious penalty, and then Temuri Ketsbaia wasting a great opening when he should have passed to the unmarked Shearer, we would have come away with a creditable draw.

You haven't completed your European education until you have played in Eastern Europe. Supporters in Budapest, Sofia, Zagreb, Kiev and Belgrade produce amazing atmospheres.

I particularly remember Belgrade, it was terrible. Usually, you don't realise the real passion of the supporters when playing because you are wrapped up in the play and then disappear down the tunnel. In Belgrade, however, I got an idea at first hand what it was like, they won and yet they still kicked off on the final whistle attacking their own police with anything they could throw! What would have happened if they had lost the tie, I cannot imagine!

Of course, I missed the game through illness but because you are only allowed so many on the bench, I was forced to walk around the perimeter of the pitch to take up my place in the crowd on the opposite side of the stadium. I remember I sat with our injured full back Steve Watson and one of our physios, we were surrounded by riot police. For our own safety, I thought rather selfishly throughout, 'I hope we don't score here.' Were we pleased to get away from that in one piece.

It was amazing, I later heard just how bad it had been. The fans were fighting among themselves all over the place and even pelted the temporary press booths at the back of the stand with bottles, celebrating as they left the stadium. Some crazy people. But to be honest I never really noticed or remember a thing during the match, the three of us just kept our heads down.

Fortunately, you are largely protected when playing and you aren't aware of what has gone on before, or even during, the matches. I was once asked whether I have to be careful not to incite certain crowds and therefore pull out of certain situations – that's rubbish! It hasn't got to the stage where football has been taken over by the hooligans. I go out and play just the same way in Zagreb or Sofia, as I do when I'm playing at home in front of our fans. I don't think about being squeaky clean on the pitch.

I like playing in Europe but there's no way I could play there permanently as some English players have done. A move to a club side abroad is something that has never appealed to me. Years ago, when I was at Charlton there was some speculation about a Dutch side, Roda JC, who were interested in signing me. I read about it in the paper, but that's as far as it got. Besides they were hardly in the big-time – I'd never even heard of them!

I like the English game, the English players, and our culture. Admittedly, I've never tried another culture so perhaps I'm not the best authority on it, but at the end of the day the Premiership is the best league in the world. All the best foreign players want to come and play here – so why go anywhere else? I wouldn't want to uproot my family either. I've got strong ties in the north-east now and I play for a massive club which I love. It would have to have been a real European giant, paying very big money to ever have prised me away from Newcastle. And at this stage in my career it's never going to happen now anyway.

A lot of British players have tried their luck in Europe over the years, and I don't care what they say, it was all motivated by money. When Alan signed for Newcastle in 1996, he had the pick of clubs all over Europe but he turned them all down in favour of his home-town club. In Alan's case though, I don't think his sense of humour would have gone down too well with some of the Spanish or Italians.

From what I've said already about our European exploits, it sounds as if we never had any luck, but this certainly seemed to be the case. If you need further proof, just look at the 1999/2000 season when we were back in Europe again, this time in the UEFA Cup. Having won in Zurich and Sofia we were drawn against the Italian side, and competition favourites, AS Roma. We went into the tie as major underdogs, written off by almost everybody, even though Bobby Robson had helped turn our whole season around. The first leg was over there and we knew that if we could hold them out in the Italian capital, then we had a great opportunity.

We gave them a real game, and they didn't like it at all, giving Alan Shearer a really rough ride. Our fans out there got really excited because although we were under pressure, as the game went on we always looked more likely to break away and score. The home side got what we all felt was a dodgy penalty when Delvecchio threw himself to the turf after a challenge from French defender Laurent Charvet.

Even back at St James' we had great chances to get that single goal back. Roma were rocking at times and with our crowd sensing this they provided some great noise which helped rattle them even more. Once again the best opportunity fell to Temuri but he was unable to lift the ball over their advancing keeper and we were out. Their celebrations on the final whistle showed just how relieved they were.

But we were far from disgraced. Our performances in Europe not long after Bobby came in and I got back my place in the first team, came as a huge boost for us all. Although we lost out to Roma we won in both Sofia and Zurich in our early UEFA Cup games. Personally, the performance in Sofia gave me a huge lift as it was part of my comeback. It was only my third appearance of the season, and this was mid-September. I was delighted to last the full match because I had earlier played just 55 minutes against Manchester United and then 65 minutes against Chelsea.

But more importantly for the club, the 2–0 win was our first victory in any competition that season. This, my first 90 minutes, came just three days before we played Sheffield Wednesday – and all our fans will remember what happened that day. We stunned The Owls with eight of the best in Bobby's first home game in charge! There was no doubt the result in Bulgaria gave the club a huge lift.

It was very noticeable that the manager had a huge knowledge of European football. His organisation of our team was so important and played a big part in helping us gain those two away wins. He knew all the opposition's players and who we should watch out for.

I do think that European competition is starting to get a bit out of hand now. We were the first English club to qualify for the Champions League having finished runners-up in the 1996/97 Premiership season, and we got a bit of stick about that. It was unfair really because we had no control over the rules, especially when you consider that Man United completed their famous Treble in 1999 by winning the Champions Cup, but they weren't reigning English league champions. Now, of course, the third-placed team in the Premiership gets in as well. It's all getting a bit silly. A European Super League is not far off now, that's the way it's going. I don't agree with it, because ultimately it will lead to the death of a lot of the smaller clubs, but it's something a club like Newcastle must get involved in if they are to prosper.

We're lucky at Newcastle to have some of the best fans around and although a European Super League would make European travel a much more regular thing, if there are any fans you can depend upon then it's the Geordies. They come in their thousands whether it's a drizzly mid-week night in Torquay, Italy or the Ukraine – they'll always turn out.

I love playing in Europe, it has a special aura. It is totally different and exciting, and sometimes a necessary relief from the Premier League. St James' is at its most intimidating on European nights. The fans want you to do well against the best teams in Europe. The atmosphere is already rocking when you get to the ground well before the kick-off. I am convinced foreign clubs find it really intimidating to play English sides in Europe. Certainly, in our case, the aristocrats of Barcelona didn't know what had hit them both on and off the pitch.

CHAPTER SEVEN

TWENTY-ONE CAPS AND SO PROUD

I suppose you can say my career has come of age after earning 21 full-international caps for England. And I truly believe I should have picked up a few more. However, I am extremely proud to have pulled on the famous England jersey, with those three lions emblazoned on the chest.

Even in my wildest dreams, as a kid growing up in Essex I never envisaged playing professional football, so the very thought of playing at international level for my country, over a six-year period, would have blown my mind completely.

Quite naturally, I remember my first cap. It came on 12 October 1994 against Romania at Wembley. I'd been in a couple of previous squads but untimely injuries had prevented me taking any part. But then my opportunity arrived courtesy of an injury to England skipper, and goalscoring talisman, David Platt. Platty had injured himself playing for Sampdoria in Italy just before the Romania international. It was great that people were beginning to compare me with such a great servant to England, and looking to me to be the ideal replacement. At the time I was scoring a lot of goals as a free-scoring midfielder – how things change!

On the Saturday before the Romania game we played Blackburn Rovers at St James' and I picked up a slight knock, but nothing too serious. KK obviously thought differently because he subbed me, although I am sure this was more to do with my performance than the actual knock. As a result there was a bit of a stink created, not by me or the manager but by the media, that Keegan didn't think I was fit enough to play.

The whole of the press wrongly picked up on this, with headlines such as 'LEE DEFIES KEEGAN OVER INTERNATIONAL DEBUT' I remember thinking at the time, what a great way to start an international career! I certainly wasn't defying anyone, especially not the man who had made this all possible in the first place. I just believed I was fit enough to play for my country.

I remember the game against Romania as if it

were yesterday. And I remember the goal as if I had just scored it. Romania were winning the game 1–0 and with half-time approaching Graeme Le Saux swung a high ball in from the left onto the head of Alan Shearer. I knew Al was going to win the header, as he had been doing that the whole game, so I set off into the Romania penalty area. I arrived at pace, controlled the ball and with the same touch took the ball past Gheorge Popescu before firing home under the advancing goalkeeper.

I'd scored for England! Should I run left or right to celebrate? But before I had time to think, BANG! I was on the Wembley turf with a smiling Ian Wright on my back, holding me down. I could not move. The rest of the game was pretty uneventful really, and I was finally substituted, on the greatest day of my career, with about 15 minutes to go.

If it makes any odds, the final score was 1–1. It didn't bother me that it was a friendly, it didn't bother me that we did not win the game, all that mattered was that I had fulfilled a boyhood dream of scoring on my England debut at Wembley.

At least I didn't get injured on my international debut. However, I wasn't so fortunate on my second international appearance, against Nigeria, on 16 November 1994, which was also at the home of football.

David Platt was fit again and, as expected, back in the team. But I managed to keep my place, playing alongside him in midfield. 'Great,' I thought. 'I'll prove we can play in the same side together.' But it didn't last long – approximately 15 minutes as I recall.

As in the Romania game, the ball came over from the flank and once again Alan won it. I got myself in the box and toe-ended it past the last defender before I shot but, just as I was about to hit the ball, which flew high over the bar, another covering player came over to challenge me. As I fell down he stamped on my hand and I just couldn't move it at all – the whole hand was limp. My first thought was that it was broken.

I had to draw attention to it in some way and when our physio came running on and took a look at it he wasn't impressed. Terry Venables had obviously seen what happened, but I remember all that went through my mind was, 'You cannot come off with only a hand injury, but nor can you stay off for too long in an international game without bringing on a sub.' No side can play with ten men, so Venables had to make the decision to replace me.

I couldn't hold my arm up at all, and I was in agony. I was taken straight away to the dressing room area before I then went off to have an x-ray. Fortunately, it was just found to be badly bruised. I had it strapped up but you can guess just how disappointing an experience it all was for me. But at least we won the game 1–0, with Platty once again scoring for his country. That was the good thing to come from the evening.

It made quite a difference to my life when I made the step up to being an international player. I got noticed more, wherever I was, even in London. I had been used to being recognised in Newcastle, that comes with playing for the Geordies, but London was always my little sanctuary. Not any more, though.

I even started getting noticed in our quiet local, The Kings Head, where I used to get asked for autographs. Most folk have enough sense, when they see you're sitting having a meal, not to bother you until you have finished. In the main, though, it's not a problem as long as they are polite. It's probably more of a pain for the people you are with.

The whole picture surrounding the launching of my international career was generally very positive. It certainly helped my confidence. I wasn't the most pushy of people before I joined Newcastle, and if you were to ask Lennie Lawrence and people at Charlton who knew me, they certainly would not have expected me to become captain of Newcastle United and, I like to think, a major player with the club.

To be honest, as a 28-year-old footballer, with two recent England caps I was in danger of getting a bit big for my boots. This was best illustrated in

January 1995 in the run up to an FA Cup third round tie against Swansea. I was carrying a knock and was called in for a late fitness test on the morning of the match.

I came through fine and assumed I would be in the starting eleven, but Keegan wasn't so sure.

'OK Rob,' he said, 'I'm going to make you sub.'

'F**k off,' I replied, 'I'm fit enough to play.'

I thought it was an insult to be left out of the team against the likes of Swansea. After all, I was *Rob Lee*, I played for England. I stormed out of St James', cursing to myself that I had been badly treated.

But over the weekend I began to see what an idiot I had been. I was not bigger that the team, and if the manager wanted to make me sub, then I should have been professional enough to have accepted it. I was ashamed of myself.

When I went in to training the following Monday I immediately apologised to Kevin. Fortunately, he put it down to experience and it was quickly forgotten. But it taught me a valuable lesson and whenever I've been made sub or left out of a squad since then, I've taken it with good grace. Kevin has certainly never forgotten the incident and whenever we meet up now he always reminds me how childish I was.

That incident was quite out of character for me because as a youngster I was always very quiet and reserved. I always believed that you were better off staying in the background. Back then I thought that if the team wasn't playing well, then I, as the youngster, would be the one dropped. It was definitely Keegan who gave me the confidence I now possess. He used to say to me, 'If you're not playing well then don't worry about it, just work hard and give the ball to someone who is.'

He always backs up this philosophy by mentioning his famous story about Cruyff and Neeskens, the great Dutch duo. It goes like this: Cruyff turns to his international team-mate Neeskens and says, 'I'm not playing well today, I'll just get the ball and I'll give it to you.' Kevin used this old example to get across the point that just because you have a bad game, you're not automatically going to be left out – all players, even great ones, play badly on occasions. That gave me great confidence.

One of the few drawbacks about becoming an international was the odd jealous comment or over-critical press report. I think this is typical of the English press, they build you up and they then want to knock you down almost straight away. They're the ones who hype you up and get you in the squad and then, after one bad game for England, it is, 'What's he doing in there? He's not an England player, he's not international standard.' Unfortunately, it's just one of those things. You have to learn to ignore it. For the most part, once I became an England player I stopped reading the match reports and articles surrounding the games, including the merit marks awarded for an individual's performance.

I've had some good, and not so good managers throughout my career, from my early years under Lennie Lawrence to my current boss Bobby Robson. At internationally level, I've been privileged to play under two wonderful managers, Terry Venables and Glenn Hoddle.

Terry is a great coach and a very good man-manager as well. He really was excellent and deserved the loyalty his players always gave him. People say I should dislike him immensely for leaving me out of two, yes two, competition squads. Everyone will obviously remember my omission from his final Euro 96 squad, but I was also left out exactly one year before, during the Umbro Tournament, against Brazil, Japan and Sweden.

Injuries permitting, I'd been in practically all of Terry's squads leading up to that end of season tournament. But then, out of the blue, I received a phone call from the England boss explaining I wouldn't be playing in the Umbro Tournament as he wanted to see Gazza, who had been out with a long term injury, play some games. I reluctantly accepted his decision and spent that summer wondering if my very short England career was over. It wasn't a very nice feeling, it left a slightly sour taste in my mouth. Mind you, that was nothing compared to what came 12 months later.

I cannot hide the fact that I expected to be in the Euro 96 squad, especially as I was playing in the games leading up to the tournament. We played Hungary at Wembley and beat them 3–1 and I thought I played okay, not spectacular, but good enough. I got a bit of a knock on my calf, but all things considered, I was feeling pretty good after the game. Obviously the press had started the speculation as to who was in and who was out, but I was very confident. How wrong I proved to be!

We were due to fly off two days later to the Far East for a short pre-tournament tour and Terry was going to name his Euro 96 squad out there. No problem, I thought. We were due to play against China first and then a Hong Kong select team. I was down on the teamsheet to play China alongside Gazza in midfield. However, my calf was still really sore the day before the game; I was trying to run it off, but it wasn't getting much better.

I told Bryan Robson and he informed the boss. Terry pulled me aside.

'How's the calf?' he asked.

'It's okay boss, just a bit sore. I'm sure it will be fine for the game.'

'Listen,' he said, 'if it's still sore leave it for this

game and get it right for the one in Hong Kong.'
Reluctantly, I agreed.

I wondered if this was a good or bad sign, so I
spoke to Peter Beardsley and told Pedro of my
concern. He brushed it off saying, 'They'll simply
be resting you. You've done well, don't worry, you'll
be in.'

We both thought we'd be involved in Euro 96
and believed we had good reason to think that. On
a number of occasions Peter had asked the England
coach if it was best for him to retire because he
hadn't played in the recent internationals. After all,
he was by then 34 years old. However, Venables on
each occasion told Pedro he still wanted him
involved with England.

Peter was eventually left out as well, which was a
shock to me. He made his feelings public that he felt
let down. To make matters worse, it was his son
Drew's birthday as well while we were away with
the squad in the Far East. This annoyed Peter, it was
as if he'd been dragged all the way out there for
nothing.

Against China, in my absence, Jamie Redknapp
came in and did well, while Nick Barmby came
into Peter's position and also put in a good
performance. But I still had no inkling that I would
be left out of the championships.

My injury, although improving, still wasn't
ready for the game against the Hong Kong select

team, which England won comfortably. Obviously, it was depressing to be on the sidelines again but I did see something the day before the game which cheered me up no end. It was the sight of Don Howe trying to explain to a bemused Steve Stone that every winger needed a trick up his sleeve. Stoney, not exactly known for his silky skills, was insistent. 'Don, I don't do tricks, I sort of bundle past players using my strength,' he said. But Don wouldn't have it and kept showing Steve his 'Stanley Matthews'. After about 45 minutes of Stoney falling over and putting in awful crosses behind the goal, Don gave up in exasperation. It just goes to show that players always know best!

But I wasn't smiling for long. The following day coach Bryan Robson came up to me and said, 'The gaffer wants to see you.' I was summoned into Terry's room and handed the bombshell.

'How's your injury?' Terry asked.

'It's fine,' I replied. 'It's not a problem, I'm OK.'

Then came the news I'd been dreading. 'You're not going to be in the squad.'

I was devastated. I didn't know what to say.

I didn't argue, I didn't smash anything up I just took it on the chin and started to walk out.

'You haven't had a good season really, Rob, have you,' quipped Terry, trying, I'm sure, to lighten the atmosphere.

It didn't work. I was close to tears as I left the

room. Newcastle had lost the league title after being 12 points clear of second-placed Manchester United and now I was left out of Euro 96. I was not going to be part of the first major soccer tournament in England since the victorious 1966 World Cup campaign.

Terry was right – it was an awful end to a promising season.

It was a long trip home, a 13-hour flight knowing I had been left out of the squad. I sat next to Pedro on the flight back, so, as you can imagine, the atmosphere was pretty gloomy.

It was the infamous flight back, yes, the Cathay Pacific flight that made all the headlines and yet I hadn't a clue that anything untoward had taken place – honest! The England party were sitting at the front of the 747 as well as in the upper deck, and I think the players who messed about must have been upstairs. However, I was oblivious to everything.

In fact, I was in a total trance on the flight all the way home. I was absolutely gutted. After I got back, I had a friend and his wife visiting me at home and they wanted to watch some of Euro 96, but I never saw any of the games. The disappointment even spilled over to affect me into the following season. I didn't play well for ages, whereas I normally start the season so well.

Up until then this was the biggest personal disappointment of my career. It was a massive blow to me. I just wasn't expecting it. People would come up to me and say, 'You should have been in,' but it was no consolation. The stark fact was that I wasn't.

I haven't seen Terry to talk to since, although when his daughter opened a pub down in Essex he sent me a letter asking if I would sort a shirt out for her. I did without hesitation. I don't dislike Terry at all, he was a great international coach. He built a good team around him off the pitch, too. I thought Bryan Robson, in particular, was excellent. He didn't do a lot of coaching because Terry did most of that, but Bryan was hugely respected by us all and acted as an ideal buffer between the players and manager. He was great for advice because he had been through it all himself as a player. He even tried to console me on the plane back from China, offering me words of comfort. Although they didn't work at the time, I am grateful to him for trying.

Whatever my feelings for Terry, Glenn Hoddle was the man who gave me a place in his France 98 squad, so I have to be thankful to him for that. Glenn was also a great coach who lost his job for non-footballing reasons.

I found out about my selection when we were out in La Manga prior to the tournament proper. It was a trip which would be remembered for only one thing – Gazza's explosive reaction to his omission from the 1998 World Cup squad.

Glenn and John Gorman decided the best way to inform the players whether they were in or out was to see us one at a time in Glenn's room. So all the names of the players on the trip were written on the notice board, with their scheduled meeting times with the boss staggered at five-minute intervals.

I don't know why the likes of Alan Shearer and other players certain to make the squad needed to go and see Glenn, but that's how it was all planned out. Each player was given a time. Mine was at 4.45 pm, Al's was at 4.40 pm and David Batty was due in after me. As I walked towards Glenn's room – it was well away from the rest of us right in another wing – there was a backlog of players all sitting in Alan's room. I went in and asked what was going on.

'Something's kicked off with Gazza,' Al replied.

We knew then and there that there'd been a commotion. It was so obvious something was up. The appointments had been postponed and John and Glenn Roeder were outside the door.

There were so many rumours flying around, they spread like wildfire that Gazza had been left out and he'd reacted by smashing up the manager's room. As time went on even more players appeared – Teddy Sheringham was the next one – and in the end there must have been about eight of us sitting in Al's room, not only wondering what had happened but also more than a little concerned about Gazza's well being.

The appointment times were well and truly out of the window by then. Gradually, sanity was restored and John came in and began calling each of us in. I remember waiting for my turn, thinking back to the morning when Batts and I had played golf with Peter 'Spuddy' Taylor, the now Leicester boss, and goalkeeping coach Ray Clemence.

Of course, the final squad details were all that anyone was thinking about by this stage, so we spent the morning trying to find out from Spuddy who was in the squad. But he was having none of it. He was winding us up, one minute saying, 'You're in,' then later saying, 'No, you're not lads, you're both out.' In the end, we'd had enough after a number of poor golf shots.

'Spuddy,' we pleaded. 'Just f***ing tell us will you. Are we in or out?'

'Well, I'll tell you what lads, you would be in *my* squad.'

He was absolutely loving it.

Anyway, suddenly it was my turn to see Glenn and I was thinking, 'What if I miss out yet again…' I looked at John just outside the door and he looked back at me winking, at least I think he was winking. 'God, I hope he's winking,' I thought, and hadn't just got something in his eye!

I need not have worried. He was winking and smiling, trying to indicate to me that I was in, that I was safe. John would often watch me both at St.

James' and in away games and always seemed to have a kind word for me. I liked John and got on very well with him.

Glenn and John were good to me, as was Terry Venables. But it was Glenn who played me the most. I thought he was a great coach and I like him and his methods very much. I didn't have any major conversations with him, but we always seemed to get on very well. His training was clearly well thought out, and that I liked. I loved the whole England experience, the training, the matches, and the camaraderie.

At first, when I was away with England, I never really enjoyed it, but it was just one of those things I wanted to do. I really wanted to prove I was good enough to play for my country. I didn't really feel part of the England setup until the Le Tournoi tournament in France. Then, we were away as a group for about six weeks and all the lads were great. I enjoyed every minute of it.

In the pre-tournament matches for the World Cup, we faced Mexico and South Africa. I played against Mexico in March 1997 when there were a lot of players out through injury. I actually played wing-back, would you believe it, for the first time in my career, certainly for England, even though I had played in so many positions. Fortunately, I had a good game and was named Man of the Match, my only one for England.

After that we went to Old Trafford where we played against a physically strong South Africa side. I scored at the opposite end to the Stratford End. I remember the game well because I so enjoyed playing with Gazza in central midfield. We stayed at Mottram Hall in Manchester before the game and had got on so well together. Gazza is a great bloke and a superb footballer. At his peak he could match the world's best – of that I have no doubt. He *was* England. He epitomised the spirit of the camp, of the nation, he just loves his football! The England squad was always a happier place with him about.

With Gazza alongside me in midfield against South Africa, I felt we played really well. I remember thinking at the time, 'This is going great' – and then it got even better as I scored, and with my left foot too!

I had a touch of flu before the game and I didn't know if I was going to play. But I was eventually given the okay ten minutes before the sides were announced – just as well, because it was one of my most enjoyable games in an England shirt.

Afterwards we travelled to Poland for a World Cup qualifier, on 31 May, a game we really had to win. Again I played in midfield with Gazza and Paul Ince. We played with three at the back and two wing-backs pushing on when the chances arose.

Gazza went off after 15 minutes after an horrendous challenge, and Batts came on in his place. Alan, inevitably, put us one-up with a superbly taken goal and then went on to have probably the finest display I've ever seen from a centre-forward, despite missing a penalty. We were under immense pressure for most of the game, breaking swiftly on the counter-attack and Alan held the ball up superbly. I remember doing just that in the last minute, going around the keeper and then cutting back and rounding him again before passing to Teddy Sheringham to make it an uncatchable score of 2–0.

Looking back now, I think the Poland game was my best performance for England, although to be fair I played very well in the Mexico game as well. It was at a time when I had my best run in the England side of three, possibly four, games. I was in the team on each occasion, although it doesn't sound like much, over a period of six months.

So everything was going well ... or so I thought! Straight after Poland we flew to France to play in Le Tournoi, but unbeknown to me I had picked up a bad toe injury. It was very painful as we arrived in France.

I didn't play in the first game against Italy, a young lad named Paul Scholes played instead! This little known ginger-haired lad came on having travelled down from Manchester United reserves.

He was absolutely outstanding against the Italians, in a class of his own. I remember thinking what a player he was going to be.

Scholesy and Ian Wright scored a goal apiece in a comfortable 2–0 win. But I couldn't enjoy the moment too much as I had to go and have an x-ray in France, at the insistence of the team doctor. Fortunately, my toe wasn't broken.

I never started any of the games at Le Tournoi, but to be fair the toe was absolutely killing me. In the end I was given only ten minutes as a sub against France. We beat them 1–0, courtesy of an Alan Shearer goal. And then I came on against Brazil, for the last half an hour or so. From then on, I felt part of the England team which was great.

Everyone felt for Gazza when we found out he wasn't in the World Cup squad. To be honest, I felt for all of the unlucky players, not just Gazza, because I'd been through the situation myself two years earlier. I knew exactly what it was like, it was a horrible, horrible feeling. At least these lads got away quickly before the press could get at them. When I was left out of the Euro 96 squad, Dennis Wise, Jason Wilcox Peter Beardsley and I had to wait until the next day before we flew home from the other side of the world. At least Gazza, Phil Neville, Dion Dublin, Ian Walker and Andy Hinchcliffe could get away quickly this time. They were put on a private plane immediately.

After we found out who was in the squad and who wasn't, I remember that Batts, Al and I jumped in a golf buggy and went across to the other side of the golf course, where we were staying, to see Kenny Dalglish. Kenny was out there with his wife Marina on holiday so we went straight to his villa and sat there in the sun having a beer. There we were, the three of us, savouring our happy moment with our Newcastle boss, but my thoughts kept wandering back to the players left out. I felt desperately sorry for them.

A lot of people in the game talk about Gazza and what a really smashing guy he is. And I agree. There are very few out there who don't like Paul once they get to know him. So what is special about the guy? It's simply his charisma. He has a real presence about him. When he walks into a room everyone immediately expects him to do something and he does, he never lets anyone down. More than anything, he is great to be around. And he'd do anything for you. He'd give you the shirt off his back if need be. He's also a great one for practical jokes, as everyone knows.

I remember once, whilst with England at the Burnham Beeches Hotel, I was about to turn in for the night. I reached to turn off the lamp, and had the fright of my life. There looking straight up at me was a giant stag beetle. It really was the biggest, blackest beetle I'd ever seen. I decided to ring a few of my England team-mates to show off my 'major' find, and perhaps have a little fun as well.

Alan, Batts and Tim 'The Cat' Flowers were at my door in a flash. They took one look at the giant insect and decided Gazza, who was still downstairs in the bar, would be our victim. We managed to capture the beetle in a glass and deposit it in Gazza's room, without too much trouble. Then we placed the beetle in the middle of his bed, got hold of Gazza's toothbrush with toothpaste, and placed it in its massive pincers. It looked remarkably like the beetle was brushing its teeth!

We rang down to the bar and spoke to our victim. 'Gazza, there's a package for you in your room.' Now, you've got to imagine the scene: four grown men, well respected England inter-nationals, hiding, like kids, in the corridor, waiting for Gazza to walk in on a stag beetle. Very mature, or what!

'Jesus Christ, what the f**k is that?' screamed Gazza. 'And it's got my f**king toothbrush!' His face was a picture as the four of us stormed in, killing ourselves with laughter.

Once we all stopped giggling like girls, Gazza grabbed the beetle and went downstairs with it, looking to create some more mayhem. On the bar there was a bowl of peanuts, so he put this monster beetle in the bowl and sat there waiting for his own unsuspecting victim.

That was Gazza all over. He could take a joke just as much as he could dish them out. He is definitely one of the funniest men I have ever met, as well as being one of England's greatest players.

Gazza is a classic example of a player who has a really bad reputation with the press, but is a diamond underneath. Paul Scholes is another who isn't known that well, because he doesn't talk much to the media. But he is a great lad and a fine player as well. Although Dave Beckham is probably the best English player I've seen – his skills are unbelievable – when you see Scholes in training, watching him go through his shooting repertoire, it's something else.

Some players are a bit lazy, like Steve McManaman and Robbie Fowler, his great pal. They used to just jog around while you'd be doing your proper warm-up. They were horrible trainers, but again, when it mattered, they did the business on the pitch. It is what happens in a match situation that really counts.

Everyone has seen how well Macca has now settled at Real Madrid and how well he performed in the Champions League final against Valencia. I've had to man mark him before so I know what he's capable of, and I can tell you he's as fit as anything.

I agree with people who say that Robbie Fowler is probably the best finisher in the English game.

He certainly is the most natural goalscorer I've seen. Nine times out of ten he hits the target, and eight times out of that nine he hits the corner of the net. I've never seen anybody do it so often. I hope he continues to do it for England for many years to come. It is an unbelievable talent that he possesses.

Of course, there is that other star of Anfield. I remember training with England on one occasion and some young kid was training with us. He was only 17 and lightning quick. Owen, I think his name was! He trained with us as if he had been doing it all his life. I thought, 'Who's this cocky git,' so, as he received a pass I went to close him down, at lightning speed. And do you know what he did? Yes, he bloody nutmegged me! Brilliant, just brilliant.

I also got on well with David Batty, having been a team-mate of his at Newcastle. It was a pity when Batts left the Toon for his hometown club Leeds. We stay in touch on the telephone, but only when I ring him! He wanted to go, and he got what he wished. So he's got no problem with then boss Ruud Gullit. He always says, 'Gullit did well for me, he got me away.' Batts continued to live on the outskirts of Leeds even when playing for us. I'm sure it must have got on his nerves doing that drive every day. He never moved when he went to Blackburn, either.

Funnily enough, he does have a very dry sense of humour, but if you didn't know him you'd think he was a bit of a lad. This could not be further from the truth. He is a genuinely funny guy, so different to the David Batty everyone knows on the pitch.

It is the same in many ways with Alan Shearer. I hear so many people accusing him of being boring, but nothing could be further from the truth! He would get up to so many tricks, especially during our time at Maiden Castle, our previous training ground. Often, if a team-mate was being interviewed outside, even if by television crew, he would not be averse to throwing a bucket of water from the first floor balcony soaking everyone in sight, including the camera team. And yet, you know what, those camera teams would come back week after week and stand in exactly the same spot!

Occasionally, the guys on the wrong end would not see the funny side. They would be complaining about how much their camera equipment was worth, but eventually they learned to film well away from the building and the flying water.

I think all footballers have got an obsession with water. I recall another incident when we were staying at the Swallow Hotel at Bisham Abbey. I was still rooming with John Beresford at the time and Alan used to share with Batts. One morning I woke up really early, about 6.30, to find there was no sign of Bez. He was out of his bed and his clothes were gone. It wasn't that unusual for him to be up at that time causing some mischief so I slowly dozed off and thought no more about it. The next thing I know, I've got the contents of a fire extinguisher full in the face. I was soaked and the bed was like a paddling pool. Then I hear the sound of Alan and Dave running down the corridor back to their room, giggling away.

About five minutes later, as I'm trying to dry myself off, Bez comes in.

'Where the hell have you been?' I said.

'Oh, I've been messing about outside, throwing stones at Alan and Batts' window.'

'You bastard,' I said, 'I've just got a soaking because of you.'

Anyway we soon got them back, we charged into their room later that morning as they were playing cards and I emptied an entire waste-paper basket of freezing water over Alan. He just sat their motionless on his bed, still holding a soaking wet hand of cards.

We've always played practical jokes on each other, but they haven't hurt anyone yet. One of the most famous incidents occurred when the tables were turned on Alan. He brought his spanking new Jaguar into training one day; it was during the good times under Keegan at Maiden Castle. Al was so proud of the car, and shall we say that everyone was aware he had it there for the first time. A few of the lads got together and decided the opportunity was too good to miss. So, with the help of one of the training ground tractors, we absolutely covered this beautiful car from top to bottom with manure and mud!

His pride and joy had been turned into nothing more than a mud heap, and how it smelled. You can guess his reaction. To say he wasn't pleased is a massive understatement. We all knew he'd get us back – and he did!

I returned to the changing rooms one lunchtime to find he'd cut the legs off my tracksuit bottoms. Batts, meanwhile, had Vaseline put on his car door handles and windscreen wipers. But it was all worth it to see Alan's face that day.

One of the quieter lads in the Newcastle camp is former England Under-21 midfielder Des Hamilton, who joined us from Bradford City a couple of years ago. Unfortunately, poor Des found himself inadvertently caught up in the middle of one of our practical jokes.

One day Alan arrived at training wearing a new top – clearly a very expensive one. To us, though, it didn't look like a designer label shirt but more like a dishcloth! Al never did have good taste in clothes, although I do think he has improved ever so slightly now. Batts and I took matters into our own hands and signed our names all over Al's shirt, in pink marker, and then we asked Des to sign it. Poor bloke, he probably thought someone had left an old shirt to be signed and he put his name on it, not realising the repercussions coming his way. Al would expect it from Batts and me, I'm sure, but never Des! He was never involved in any shenanigans, always being careful not to offend anyone. But Des panicked when he realised what he had actually signed was Al's designer shirt!

We knew Al would at some stage get us all back, it could be a day it could be a month, but he was definitely going to get his revenge. But Des didn't realise how far Al would go.

Anyway, Des went back to the dressing room to get his gear one lunchtime, only to find it was completely in shreds. He had to walk out with his training gear still on. He left the ground in a state of shock and all he could do was keep repeating, 'You're bloody mad you lot, you're all bloody mad!' Needless to say, he's never got involved again since.

So life with both England and Newcastle is never dull and that goes for the managers too. The departure of Glenn Hoddle was for me a sad time, because I had, and still have, the utmost respect for the man and for his coaching. The whole thing surrounding his working relationship with Eileen Drury was blown out of all proportion, in my opinion. All the time I was there with England, Glenn never once said to me, 'Go and see Eileen Drury, Rob.' He was more likely to have said, 'If you want to use her, she's there to be contacted.' But he never forced anyone to go.

We had another fellow, a Dr Yann Rougier, who would come along to help us out during the World Cup. It was appropriate as he was a French doctor specialising in diet advice.

He came with a great reputation. The previous season he worked with Arsene Wenger during Arsenal's double-winning campaign. Tony Adams and the rest of the Arsenal lads in the England squad had a great deal of respect for him. I suppose Glenn thought if it worked for them, why not for us.

The doctor was concerned we ate the right things, and at the right time of the day. He made sure we took the correct supplements – we took a lot of these during the World Cup, like potassium straight after training. It was horrible, but we had to drink it with our meal. We had to eat a yoghurt first, and then the main meal, and then we took these tablets. I am certain it did us no harm.

Some people also took Creatine, if they wanted it, but you didn't have to. I didn't touch it. Although I took all the other supplements, it was different to what we were used to. Still, there was no problem with any of the players, as far as I could tell.

I didn't read the article in *The Times* that eventually led to Glenn's departure, but my feelings were one of regret and sorrow – sorrow because England were losing a very fine coach. He had obviously said something out of line, but if you've spoken to him you know he's a caring person – I don't believe he would have meant his comments about disabled people to come out as they did, that invalid folk deserved to be in wheelchairs. He wouldn't mean it like that because he's not that sort of person. He's really a decent bloke.

I just felt he was hounded out. And not because of his results on the field, because I think we would have qualified for the European Championships anyway, even though we were made to pay for costly mistakes by Sweden. And his record as England coach wasn't that bad. He was obviously sacked because of very different reasons.

I feel at certain times the media can almost dictate whether a manager, certainly an England manager, goes or stays.

I expected my international swansong would be France 98, so I went there to enjoy every moment. And although I only played 17 minutes of one game, against Colombia, to be involved even to that degree is a memory I will never forget. No-one can take that away from me.

Although I wasn't going to announce, officially, that I was going to retire from international football, I had decided that if I wasn't selected in Glenn Hoddle's first squad for the Euro 2000 qualifiers I would pack it in. Fortunately, I made the squad, even though it wasn't for long!

The first murmurings of Glenn's possible sacking came after the defeat against Sweden, in the first match of the Euro 2000 qualifiers. In the next qualifying game, against Bulgaria at Wembley, I was selected to play in my now favoured holding role. Unfortunately, we failed to win. Two days later we travelled to Luxembourg for our next qualifier, one which the whole country expected us to win com-fortably. That we did, but it was anything but comfortable. Glenn brought me on 20 minutes from time in what was to be my 21st and final England appearance.

The funny thing was, in the dressing room after the game the boss was reading the riot act to certain players but he actually praised me. He said, 'Rob Lee's come on for 20 minutes and showed more determination and more effort than a lot of you did in the whole game.'

How ironic that the infamous *Times* newspaper article brought an end not only to Hoddle's England career but also my own.

Of course, after Glenn came Kevin Keegan, a man I knew well! Because of the high esteem in which Keegan held me while he was at Newcastle saying I was, among other things, the best midfielder in the country, I suppose it was natural that a lot of people thought his appointment as England manager would reignite my international career. But I have to admit that was never something that I thought about. I certainly wouldn't have wanted an England recall under those circumstances anyway, if people said I had got back into the side just because of my old pal's act with Keegan.

At any rate I was 33 at the time, and I'd already played 21 times for my country, and I think it was a case of needing to blood some new young midfield players. We have got so many talented youngsters coming through now – the likes of Lee Bowyer and Joe Cole to name only two – and they have got to be given games to get the experience they need for the big occasion.

The calls for my England recall got louder when I eventually won back my place in the Newcastle team, having been sidelined for so long under Gullit, but realistically I would have only expected a run out if there had been a glut of injuries.

Of course, it would have been a great honour to have had another chance to shine for my country, but now, at international level at least, my time is up.

CHAPTER EIGHT

FALL OF THE MESSIAH

At the start of the 1996/97 campaign there was no hint of the dramatic events which would take place off the field, leading to the departure of 'The Messiah,' as the fans had christened Kevin Keegan, and the arrival of Kenny Dalglish in mid-January.

On the field we welcomed the arrival of the world's most expensive player, Alan Shearer, for £15 million and after a shaky opener at Everton we were flying high in first place in the league towards late November.

However, after a near disastrous run which saw us go seven games without a win, we had slumped to sixth by Boxing Day evening. Although we put matters right with a 7–1 hammering of Spurs and a 3–0 defeat of Leeds United, Kevin had seen enough. He departed in dramatic fashion on 8 January, 1997 after five wonderful years at Newcastle. He was replaced, six days later, by Kenny Dalglish, co-incidentally the same man who had replaced the irreplaceable KK as a player for Liverpool nearly 20 years earlier.

Dalglish somehow took us back up the league and we finished in a hugely creditable runners-up spot in the table which ultimately led to our first ever appearance in the Champions League – and yet KD got too little praise for this history-making achievement in my view.

Going back to the start of that season, when we returned for pre-season training the place was buzzing as usual. At the time Kevin and chairman Sir John Hall were rumoured to be interested in every world-class striker – Gabrielle Batistuta and Shearer being just two of the stars linked with a move to the rejuvenated Tyneside.

At Heathrow Airport Kevin stepped off a plane bound for Bangkok, where the squad were heading on a three-game Far East tour, to complete the deal which left the whole footballing world, and certainly Manchester United boss Alex Ferguson (who had seemed poised to sign Shearer) amazed and bewildered. On 29 July England hero Shearer signed for his hometown club Newcastle before jetting out to the Far East to meet up with his new clubmates in Singapore.

So Kevin was anything but downcast. In one fell swoop he had emphasised just how big Newcastle's ambitions were. He was excited, about his new signing and the club's future. As far as the players were concerned we knew that the board's willingness to put their hands in their pockets and pull out £15 million for the world's best striker said one thing – they were 100 per cent behind the manager in everything he was doing.

So, to later learn of a number of disagreements Kevin had with certain members of the board, possibly Sir John's son Douglas in particular, came as a huge shock. We didn't realise that certain directors might have been a little put out by the way KK took all the praise for Shearer's signing, offering little thanks to the men who actually set up and settled the negotiations and transfer fee. But surely if there was any sort of undercurrent of unrest, they wouldn't have paid out £15 million on Kevin's say-so in the first place.

The size of the fee didn't shock me or the rest of the players. The club had been able to find the money to sign Les Ferdinand for £6 million, Warren Barton for £4 million, David Ginola for £2.5 million and Tino Asprilla for £7.5 million, so we knew at the time that Newcasle United had plenty of cash.

Before Al signed we heard rumours the fee would be £10 million and then £12 million, and all of a sudden it was £15 million. Keegan had always said he wanted the best players and no matter what they cost he seemed able to go out and get them.

Al was immediately welcomed by the players. He flew out to Singapore with club photographer Ian Horrocks but then returned home, while the rest of the squad flew on to Osaka in Japan. Obviously, I'd met Alan before through England squads and knew what a superb player he was, but there was certainly no sign of us becoming the great friends that everybody knows us to be now. In fact, after our first brief 'hellos' in the corridors of the England hotel, I thought he was anything but friendly. Aloof, yes, arrogant, possibly, but friendly? Definitely not.

Mind you, he later told me he thought the same of me! What's that they say about great minds thinking alike?

Anyway, we would have loved to have joined him on that plane home to England, because we were feeling very tired well before the end of the promotional tour. Without any doubt whatsoever, our early season form suffered because of it.

Whether the club went due to pressure from sponsors or to further lift their profile, as Manchester United have done since, I don't know, but it was too long a trip. It didn't give us enough time to get back, have a rest and get ready for the start of the Premiership season.

On the first day of the new season we went to Everton, with not one of our players playing well. We lost pretty comfortably. Big Duncan Ferguson and Gary Speed scored for them in our 2–0 defeat. We'd made the start we didn't want or need. The confidence was such that we expected to win at Goodison, yet all this result did was to put us on the back foot from the off.

Alan delighted the Geordies by getting off the mark in the following game with a wonderful free-kick against Wimbledon. At least he'd begun well but the team's start was very inconsistent. After this we lost at Sheffield Wednesday before visiting Sunderland, when only a hundred or so of our fans actually got in.

We were towards the bottom of the table and they were going quite well at the time, but we put on a great performance and won 2–1 with goals from Peter Beardsley and Les Ferdinand. It got our season going and from then we had a great run of results and we were soon in second place behind Man United … again!

However, the thinnest of cracks began appearing. Then things got progressively worse, reaching an all-time low on Boxing Day. We visited Blackburn and didn't play well at all to lose 1–0. The defeat saw us drop to sixth. In the dressing room after the game Kevin was not a happy man, to put it politely. He had a few choice words to say to a few of the players – his criticism of Les, in particular, was later highlighted. Obviously, Les, like a few of us, didn't play well but it seemed Kevin was quicker to have a go than normal. One of Keegan's favourite sayings when he was giving us a rollicking was, 'If I'd told you to go out there and do nothing, then you've done exactly what I asked for!' and I think Les took exception to that.

Significantly, Kevin did say something which I'd certainly never heard from him before. 'Maybe I'm losing a few of you,' he said. 'If I can't get you to play for me anymore, I might as well not be here.'

He wasn't *losing* anybody. The players still loved and respected him without question. I think it was his own frame of mind more than anything, presumably caused, as we found out later, by the hitches he was having behind the scenes.

I didn't think too much of his outburst because he had acted that way before. He used to get the hump for a few days but it always tended to blow over. But the thing that really made me think all was not well in the 'Keegan wonderland', was his reaction to our 7–1 thrashing of Spurs at St James'. Keegan used to love us playing great attacking football and giving teams a 'good hiding'. On this day we played Spurs off the park with some wonderful flowing football. We scored seven but it could have been ten!

Al was magnificent that day and he, Les and yours truly each scored a couple – we were unstoppable. I thought, 'Great, that'll cheer the gaffer up, just the sort of game he loves.'

I was sure when we walked into the dressing room that he'd be flying and come out with one of his tongue-in-cheek comments, like 'What do you call that lads? If that's the best you can do, I'm wasting my time!', then turn to Terry Mac and burst out laughing. But on this occasion, it was different. He was pleased but appeared to be thinking more about how the Spurs boss Gerry Francis was feeling after his team's heavy defeat, rather than our magnificent win.

At the time I just thought he must be having an off day, I never in a thousand years thought he'd leave the club. He *was* Newcastle. He was all I knew, and I couldn't imagine him without Newcastle and Newcastle without him. Of course, we'd heard rumours about bust-ups behind the scenes, but no-one in life agrees 100 per cent about everything. I couldn't believe it would be serious enough to cause him to leave.

None of it made sense to me. Only three months before, the board had given him £15 million to spend on one player. Why would they do that if there were ructions behind the scenes? I think the

Keegan factor was one of the main reasons why Alan signed for the club. Keegan was his idol as well as mine. Alan could have signed anywhere, he had his choice of clubs all around Europe.

He must have been really shocked when KK left. When he first signed he would have asked about the future plans of the club. I don't think he'd have signed if Kevin told him he'd be leaving in six months! However, Kevin is his own man and obviously things were happening which made it impossible for him to stay on.

He eventually walked out in the aftermath of an FA Cup tie at, of all places, The Valley, on 5 January. We went into training aware of the rumours that he'd gone. I was shell-shocked, the day was just going past me in a blur. I couldn't take it in, I was deeply upset.

I'd been here five years then, but if it had happened after one or two years, having said I'd signed for him rather than the club, I probably wouldn't have stayed at Newcastle, I'd probably have followed him. However, by this time I had become attached to the club, got on very well with the fans, and got on well with the people at the club, so it was slightly different.

Anyway, Terry Mac and Arthur Cox got us all in a room upstairs at the training ground at Maiden Castle. Terry said Kevin had gone but he didn't give us any reasons as to why.

I don't think at the time he knew. It was just put down to circumstances. Terry was very upset. I even noticed a little tear in his eye. He was a good friend of Kevin's as well – he'd been brought to Newcastle by Kevin after all – and he was devastated.

Terry and Coxy were put in charge for the next game while the club looked for a suitable replacement. I wondered what the new 'duo' would say before the game. I needn't have worried because out of the shadows stepped Arthur 'Churchill' Cox. I name him after the great war-time leader because of his wonderful speech at a time of crisis as he and Terry prepared us for the next game, Aston Villa away. Unfortunately it was a game I would miss through suspension.

It was a great pre-match speech, very moving, with the emphasis on 'doing it for Kevin.' The lads really loved it and within a few minutes of the start, we were 2–0 up. How's that for motivation? Unfortunately, Villa came back into the game to force a deserved draw. But there was a real united feeling among the players, those on the bench, and the fans.

It was a difficult time for the club because we had lost our 'Messiah', the man who had led us to the heights where we were now.

We didn't know who was coming in to replace Kevin. You are paid to be professional and you cannot allow things like that to affect your performances. Of course, there was a lot of speculation but the only people who knew were the chairman and the board. All we hoped was that the person who came in would continue what Kevin Keegan had started.

Although both Al and David Batty had enjoyed playing for Kenny Dalglish at Blackburn they had no prior contact with him. The first we knew was when Dougie Hall called a few of us into the ground. He told the then players' committee of myself, Les, Alan, Peter, Lee Clark and John Beresford that Kenny was coming in as manager.

Alan had already told me not to believe whatever I had seen or read about Kenny, that he was actually a good laugh and good fun to be with and a fine manager. And, I got on well with him from the word go.

I was suspended for his first game in charge. It was the FA Cup replay with Charlton at St James'. I had scored the last goal during Kevin's reign which gave us a 1–1 draw at The Valley.

Kenny's welcome from the fans was un-believable, not lukewarm as many have since intimated. They were ready to give him their full support, because loyalty is one of their greatest strengths. The fans welcome every new manager, especially if they believe he can take the club up to the next level. To be fair, Kenny had a good record and should have done.

We ended the season superbly, finishing second and qualifying automatically for the Champions League. The only real change I remember with the arrival of Kenny was that instead of five-a-side goals in training, we now had full-sized goals. I think this was because 'King Kenny' loved joining in the training, as did Keegan before him. I think he found it much easier to curl the ball into the top corner with bigger goals!

I know the impression is that everything was changed when Kenny came in, that we stopped smiling and enjoying ourselves, but this is complete rubbish. He certainly didn't try to restrict the way we played for the final four and a half months of that season.

CHAPTER NINE

KING KENNY

After his first six months in charge as manager of Newcastle United, Kenny Dalglish set about putting his own stamp on the club. He was determined to reinstate reserve team football, which had been scrapped by Kevin Keegan. He also decided to make training a far less open event.

He had learned from his Blackburn Rovers days that it is not only the public who turn up to watch your side train, but that other less desirable onlookers can ensure that team tactics and other secrets make their way back to the opposition camps.

Kenny preferred privacy for training, in contrast to Kevin's open-door ethic and while, to be fair, the pitches were superb at Maiden Castle it was still a University-owned sports centre. Because of this we had no privacy in the dressing rooms, we had no privacy anywhere really.

Despite this, I think it was a mistake to move to our new training complex at Chester-le-Street, in the shadow of Durham County Cricket Club's Riverside Ground, because our new facilities are very poor in comparison to those at Maiden Castle. Sure, it has a degree of privacy but the pitches are of a Sunday league standard. It is like a park, really. There's bits of rubbish everywhere and even dogs' mess on the grass – as our Greek international George Georgiadis found out one day when he put his hand in a freshly dumped crap whilst doing sit-ups! It certainly made the lads double up with laughter. George never did see the funny side of that. I'm sure he would have preferred our superb pitches at Maiden Castle.

I think if a foreign player is coming to sign for a club of the stature of Newcastle, they must assume that we have a great training ground, but I will put a pound to a penny that we have the worst facility in the whole of the Premier League. Not only is it poor, we don't even own the ground.

Before the FA Cup semi-final against Chelsea in 1999/2000, we practised at Arsenal's training complex. It was, as Bobby Robson would say, unbelievable. One of the pitches even has under soil heating! The Gunners must have 10–15 pitches in total, all to the exact same measurements as

Highbury. The complex also had a swimming pool, a massive gym and a fully-equipped medical centre.

Ever since I joined Newcastle in 1992, I was told by Kevin and Sir John Hall that we were having a training ground and complex built. They even showed us where it was going to be, hinting that we might want to live there so we were close by. But Woolsington, a suburb of Newcastle six miles from the centre of the city, has never materialised. I keep hoping though. A club of our size really should have a great training complex to match.

In these terms we are miles behind Man United, who have just recently moved to a new one. Even my old club Charlton have their own. Surely it is important for our kids and reserves to be able to train with the senior players, rather than training a good few miles away as they do now. I think our youth academy should get used to seeing the likes of Alan Shearer, Gary Speed and the other internationals and actually have the opportunity some days to train with them. Mind you, they are probably training on better pitches than us at the moment – no bobbles, no rubbish and more importantly no dogs' mess.

Returning to those twenty months when Kenny was in charge, things began to go wrong after an excellent opening spell at the back end of the 1996/97 season, when the new signings started to arrive during that summer.

I still believe that Lady Luck did not deal Kenny a good hand at St James' Park and that the supporters are not so condemning of him as many have made out. He probably got most things right, from the juniors and academy up to the reserves, but it was the performance of his first-team squad which was of most importance to the fans.

The summer was a very busy time: we sold David Ginola and Les Ferdinand to Spurs, Robbie Elliott to Bolton; and we signed Stuart Pearce, Ian Rush and John Barnes on free transfers and Alessandro Pistone from Inter Milan for £4.3 million. We also signed Danish international Jon Dahl Tomasson from Dutch club Heerenveen for 2.2 million that July.

I believe Kenny had it going on the right lines, but allowing Les to go to Spurs was a mistake, in my opinion. Whoever was at fault for that bit of business, I will always maintain that it was a major mistake in the recent history of the club.

Alan and Les were the best striking partnership I have seen anywhere, without any doubt. To break that up after they had scored 49 goals between them in the previous season was crazy. Whether there were other things going on, such as Les wanting to go, or whether the club wanted to get their money back for a player who was approaching 31, I'm not sure. But were they really going to get anyone better to replace him at that sort of price? I didn't think so.

Despite this, everything looked rosy for the start of the season, with the new signings settling in nicely. I even picked up my first trophy as skipper, after we won a pre-season tournament in Dublin. Tomasson, especially, was on fire in those games as I recall. He was lively, took some great positions and finished well, but I always had this little doubt, after training with him, that he didn't quite have the physical stature to be a success in the Premiership. My reservations were simply that he was very lightweight. Although he was doing extremely well pre-season, with some great goals, and he was mixing well with the lads, I felt he needed to put on some muscle.

But then, just as Les was tying up his move to White Hart Lane, Alan picked up a serious injury in another pre-season tournament, this time at Goodison Park, a ground which has never been good to us early season. Hours after Pistone completed his move from Serie A, we were involved in the Umbro Tournament. During the game against Chelsea, Al went down in a heap with nobody remotely near him. I knew he was hurt badly, our big balding Geordie, as I call him, doesn't stay down unless it's something very serious.

Within hours he was having major surgery to

repair his badly damaged ankle ligaments. On that same day, 27 July, I tried to persuade Les to call off his £6 million move to Spurs.

I remember we were travelling back from Merseyside and Warren Barton, a close friend of Les, was speaking to him on the phone, so I grabbed the mobile and pleaded with Les.

'Any chance of you coming back, Les? We certainly need you now.'

'Sorry, Rob, it's too late, it's all done,' he replied.

Obviously, the spirits right throughout the club took a dive with the news about Al. One doctor said he'd be out only five weeks, but then news filtered through that it was going to be nearer eight months. Naturally, all of Kenny's plans were up in smoke there and then. Al's injury would have been a massive blow even before Les' move, but now? It was a massive responsibility for Jon Dahl and Tino Asprilla to carry.

However, we still believed that if we could get off to a good start, we had half a chance of doing well, and to be fair we did. Tino, although in and out, was still capable of wonderful things. Everyone hoped he could carry us and play on his own up front, which he did on a number of occasions.

Tino was a real character. My first memory of him was seeing him freezing to death huddled in a full-length fur coat walking to St James' Park. But it wasn't even mid-winter! I thought somebody had better tell him that it gets colder than that in the north!

But he came in and everyone loved the guy, and although he didn't speak any English at first and used to call the lads by their surnames, which pissed us off a bit, he soon picked up the Geordie lingo with the help of his interpreter.

The interpreter, a guy called Nick, was a good lad too. He would accompany him everywhere although the rumour that circulated at the time about him even coming into the showers after the game was rubbish! Nights out with Tino were always entertaining especially if he wanted to chat up the ladies because Nick would have to do the talking. We always had to speak to him through his interpreter. Tino was just a very funny man, and the more he got to grips with the English language, which he was learning very quickly, the funnier he became.

As I've said, he was a quick learner, but not quick enough. We used to have some fun with him. I don't know how many times he got into trouble because of us. Whenever he asked us when training was, we used to tell him the wrong time and place, so he'd always turn up late. Keegan would be going bloody spare with him, and the same would be the case with Kenny.

Mind you, usually when Tino was late it was all his own doing. He was a nightmare for oversleeping. In fact, the only time I remember him arriving early for training was when the clocks went forward, which again, the lads forgot to mention. Keegan couldn't believe his eyes when he saw Tino, fully changed, boots and all, wandering around trying to work out why he was the only player in sight. KK didn't stop laughing for weeks.

Although we were always winding him up, Tino never lost his temper. He will always hold a special place in the hearts of all true Newcastle fans and his former team-mates.

Wherever Tino plays his football those fans will see moments of skill which they may never see again in their lifetime. And when I finish playing I am certain that this particular Colombian will be high on my ratings' list of former team-mates, when it comes to ability on the field and the capacity to make us all laugh off it.

Tino certainly proved his worth on the opening day of the 1997/98 season. We defeated Sheffield Wednesday 2–1 with a couple of great goals from him. But we should have had it wrapped up more convincingly. Having been scoring for fun pre-season, Jon Dahl missed a sitter in the first 45 seconds – the good start, which I felt KK needed, was in tatters. His confidence, I believe, started to desert him after that miss. If he had scored in that first minute, he might have become a legend on Tyneside, the fans would have loved him. The difference between success and failure in football is often such a thin line.

He didn't do very well for Newcastle in the end. I was very disappointed for him, because I saw he had something about him. But I wish him all the best. He has gone to Feyenoord in Holland and done very well. He has also enjoyed success in the Champions League, too, and has proved he can score goals.

The loss of Shearer and an off-form Tomasson weren't the only problems faced by Kenny. He had his difficulties with the media too. He spoke to them, of course, but only allowed them to know what he wanted them to know. Some managers will allow themselves to be pushed around by the media but Kenny wouldn't. During that season the press wanted him to have a go at a few of his players, but he simply wouldn't. That was something he never did.

We all respected him for this. He was taking all sorts of flak and still he wouldn't say the players let him down. We were thrashed 4–1 at Leeds and we were awful, yet he still took the flak. He gave us a right good hiding in the dressing room, but what was said behind closed doors always stayed there.

Kenny wouldn't show his emotions, but I know he liked the area and loved the club. I think he was desperate to be a success here. He still has feelings towards the club and when you hear him on television he is always very positive about Newcastle.

During his time at St James' he was very good to me. He handed me the captaincy, a great honour, and was very supportive, but to be honest he was like that for all of his players. Probably because of his past relationship with Alan, a lot of people thought he would give the captaincy straight to him, but Kenny stuck by me.

Hopefully, I never let him down. But can all his signings look in the mirror and honestly say the same? I doubt it. I hope they took a long look at themselves after his departure in August 1998. Tomasson and Swedish international Andreas Andersson were two, certainly. The Swede looked impressive on his debut at Aston Villa but he seemed to go downhill from there. His form was poor and he seemed to spend a lot of the time injured.

I have always said that it was his players who ultimately let Kenny down. I know Ruud Gullit went on about some division between the British and foreign players at the club, but I can honestly say this has never been the case. Obviously, you are going to get foreign players talking and mixing more with their fellow countrymen, but when we went out on a social we certainly didn't say, 'Hey, we are not inviting him!'

Listen, we are grown men. We don't have to like

each other off the pitch, but as long as you respect each other on it, what is the problem? I never disliked any of my team-mates, but some of them I lost respect for because of the way they played. As players I think some could have done better for Newcastle. Remember, this is a great football club with a history and tradition, and fans who live from match to match wanting only one basic thing – that the players respect them and give their all for the club.

So were those twenty months wasted? I don't believe so. Kenny started the academy, he set up the reserve team again. I don't think that was a waste of time. But Newcastle United FC stood still for a couple of years when people expected us, following on from Keegan, to move on up. I have said many a time we were still years behind Man United.

True, we went from second in Kenny's first part-season to finish 13th in his only full season in charge, and yet during that time we qualified for, and then did okay in, the Champions League and made an FA Cup final appearance. So it wasn't all bad. Quite honestly, I would say the real heart of the problem was the injury to Alan. You can cope for a few games without your best striker, but over a season if you miss your main goalscorer for months on end, you will struggle. And that is exactly what we did.

There were also problems off the field, notably a couple of major PR blunders, such as the incident surrounding our fourth-round FA Cup tie with non-league Stevenage Borough. Although this made great copy for some of the national newspapers, it was very bad for Newcastle United. It soon turned us from being one of the most popular clubs in the country to one everyone disliked.

Yet while we took some stick for the way we handled the Stevenage game, the players felt the club had handled things correctly. We were getting the piss taken out of us, really. It all started when the club offered to play the game at St James'. What big club doesn't offer to do that? We genuinely felt we were giving Stevenage the chance to earn some money through a guaranteed bigger crowd. However, they took the hump with that.

Some of the things they came out with in the press, about us not being a professional club, were outrageous. I don't remember all the comments but after the first game we wanted to ram them back down their throats! It was Al's first game back after injury and he scored really early on, within two minutes, but it was always going to be tough, because of the pitch and the way the tie had been built up. I'd played non-league football and knew Stevenage would battle for everything. And everyone was rooting for them. It seemed, probably for the first time ever, like the world was against us. And of course they equalised and took us to a replay at St James'. Because of all the adverse publicity we had, which I believe was not all our fault, it appeared everyone wanted us to lose. They got sponsorship from *The Sun,* their players were pictured with *Sun* footballs; elsewhere Graham Roberts even got the sack as Yeovil boss for supporting us, saying that Stevenage were not liked within non-league circles. But the fact is we let the smallest player on the pitch score with a header, which was absolute crap play on our part. However, we remained very confident that we'd get the job done at St James' Park.

I do give the Stevenage players credit, though, for the way they played, that's something I want to get over. But it was the FA Cup. The important thing when you're playing away from home is not to get beat, no matter who the opposition is. We'd seen Coventry City get beat by Sutton United a few years earlier. In one game anyone can beat anyone! We won the replay but from then on we were public enemy number one, and Kenny took the brunt of it through to the final.

The situation wasn't helped by our poor league form. I remember we were due to play Crystal Palace at home in a game that, if I got booked, I would miss the FA Cup semi-final against Sheffield United. Kenny pulled me to one side and said, 'I'd rather not risk you.' I knew he'd give me a right bollocking if I played and got a yellow card, so I left it to him. I didn't play and we lost. The ironic thing is that in the following game we went to Southampton, ten days after I was left out against Palace. The Dell was a major bogey ground for us. We were actually beating them 1–0 with a rare goal from yours truly and things were looking good. But it was all about to change very quickly as I chased my good friend and ex team-mate John Beresford for a loose ball, and I felt my hamstring pull. Me? Pull a hamstring? Surely that only happens to quick players.

I came off devastated, knowing I would miss the semi-final. To make matters worse, Southampton scored two late goals to beat us 2–1.

Although I missed the semi-final defeat of Sheffield United at Old Trafford, at least I was fit, and free from suspension, to play in the club's first FA Cup final in 24 years. But that's where the good news ended, as Arsenal, already League champions, deservedly completed the double against us as we chose the wrong day to play badly. We were clearly below par at Wembley. In my opinion, it was probably the first time Kenny had got his tactics wrong. We had been playing five at the back, with three centre-halves, for the majority of the second half of the season, but all of a sudden he changed it days before the final.

He was worried about the speed of Marc Overmars so he chose to put Alessandro Pistone to right-back to combat the Dutchman's pace. However, it seemed a strange thing to do as Pistone was almost exclusively left-footed. Warren Barton came in at left back, and we played 4–4–2. When we met up with the England lads a week later, Tony Adams said to me, 'We couldn't believe it! We were working all week on how to combat five at the back and you played 4–4–2.'

Sandro got some stick for not using the space he had to contribute to our attacks, but he was just not comfortable in that right-side position. And obviously he was worried about Overmars. In the end, that is how they got their first goal. Pistone made a mess of things, getting himself the wrong side of the Dutchman when chasing a hopeful long ball, Overmars latched on to it and shot past Shay Given. It killed us really. Kenny had his reasons for playing that formation, but it didn't work on the day.

So another summer arrived and we all wondered what would happen and what new players, if any, would come in. Stephane Guivarc'h arrived from Auxerre after a victorious World Cup final campaign, as did German international midfielder Dietmar Hamann from Bayern Munich. All we'd seen of the Frenchman was a stack of goals he'd scored previously at both international and club level, which you have to admit was impressive. I found his style similar, but nowhere as good, as

Alan's. Guivarc'h simply wasn't quick, and he wasn't great in the air either, but even so you could still see he was a natural goalscorer. I thought if he scored 25 goals in the season for us, I wouldn't complain.

Kenny also signed several youngsters such as Garry Brady, who cost £650,000 from Spurs, Paul Robinson and James Coppinger from Darlington, Des Hamilton from Bradford City, Andy Griffin from Stoke as well as his own son Paul – all players for the future.

What Kenny was trying to do was get some young players in quickly because we had none in the reserves, and so few coming through. He knew he had a good first-team squad, and a good first eleven, but he didn't have much behind it. He wanted young players to start building for the future of Newcastle, bringing them in whenever he could, just as Leeds United are doing with such success now.

One of the questions I am often asked is whether it's right that Kenny should take all the blame for our slump in fortunes, or does Kevin Keegan have to carry some of the can. I'd say it was a bit of both. I can understand Kevin's reasons for his scrapping of the reserve team. The way we played football, we needed a good pitch. At the time, the reserve team played a certain amount of reserve team games at St James'. Because the Milburn, Sir John Hall and

Gallowgate Stands were having extra tiers built to increase the ground's capacity, less sunlight was reaching the playing surface, and the pitch was getting worse and worse every year.

Kevin believed that the more games played on it, the worse it would get and it was going to affect the way we play. You've got to understand, though, that we had signed inexperienced players like Darren Huckerby and Chris Holland, who turned out to be good buys, but at that time they had nowhere to play.

So it was a Catch-22 situation. I think Kevin was pushed into a corner and he wouldn't back down. I think he wanted to play all the games at our reserve ground, at Gateshead Stadium, rather than just the majority. The FA had a rule at the time, which has since been scrapped, that a certain number of reserve matches had to be played where the first team played. Kevin obviously said to the FA, 'If you don't allow us to play there, I'll pull my team out.' Eventually, that's what he did. That was the way he was, he would do things on impulse.

So when Kenny came in he obviously had to rebuild and quickly. He saw the need for young players to guarantee the future of the club. Kenny's legacy of buying good young players is still visible now. He also went to the other end of the spectrum by signing players with vast experience behind them, such as John Barnes, Ian Rush and Stuart Pearce – legends one and all!

Pearcey was an excellent signing, I thought. Although not suited to playing left-back anymore, as a central defender he was still an outstanding player. Along with John 'Digger' Barnes, Stuart was a major influence in the dressing room – apart from his taste in music, that is. The Stranglers and Sex Pistols was not quite my scene!

Pearcey was brilliant. He knew most of the players, and certainly all of us respected him, so he had no problems settling in. He was very quiet off the field. He used to have a big farm in Nottinghamshire, so he didn't move up to live in the area, but he did rent a flat in Durham. He spent most of the time after his lease ran out trying to cadge a bed for the night off one of the lads.

At the start of the 1998/99 season we travelled to the Republic of Ireland, twice, to play some warm-up games. And everything was going well, especially against Bray Wanderers, in the lovely seaside town south of Dublin, until Guivarc'h went over on his ankle as he crossed for Alan. Unfortunately he had to be carried off the field by our physio Derek Wright.

The Frenchman missed a month with an ankle injury – and did not start a single League game for Kenny before he was sacked! Actually, he only started two matches in the League before being transferred to Glasgow Rangers by Ruud Gullit.

There was quite a lot of speculation before the first League game of the season at home to my former club Charlton, as to who would play in midfield. Kenny had bought Hamann, and he also had Batty, Gary Speed and myself. We were all central midfield players, of course, and everyone wondered which one, or maybe two players, weren't going to play. But Kenny had other ideas.

He played a diamond formation, with myself on the right, Speedo on the left and Hamann playing in front of Batts just behind Alan and Stephane. It worked well, as it had in a pre-season friendly win over Juventus at St James' Park. We were looking forward to a great season, especially as we had Al fit.

And I don't think it started that badly in what proved to be Kenny's final two games at the club. We were never in danger of losing to Charlton, but we couldn't score and it ended goalless. In hindsight, we all knew Charlton were a difficult side to beat, especially at the very start of the season. But we took a lot of stick for our performance in that match, Kenny in particular, and everyone started calling for his head.

You could hear the grumblings from the crowd. We then went to Chelsea and got what I thought was a great draw. Obviously, other people thought differently!

Again, as with Keegan, none of the players were aware things were coming to a head. Prior to the

Charlton game I had signed a new three-year contract, so I certainly wasn't aware of any problems with the gaffer. I wanted to play for Kenny and I wouldn't have signed it if I had known he was going to have been replaced as manager within days.

We hadn't exactly had a run of bad results, although that shouldn't have surprised me because neither had Keegan, but I found Kenny's departure amazing and very disappointing. You can understand it if your manager is getting poor results. I half expected Ruud to get the chop after our performances under him, but certainly not Kenny and Kevin.

Once again it was Terry McDermott who was given the task of telling us all, but I think once he knew Ruud was coming in as replacement he didn't want anything to do with it. In the end Kenny called us in and explained what had happened. You could tell by his words and by the way he was acting that he was bitterly disappointed, especially as we had yet to lose a game that season.

I would sum up Kenny's time at the club as a transitional period. I think he took over at a bad time. Although people didn't realise it, off the pitch the club was going through a few changes, especially with it becoming a public limited company, and other upheavals in the boardroom. The upshot of this was that decisions such as transfer deals had to be ratified by the two boards which meant a delay in being able to move quickly for a player. Then other decisions were being announced through the Stock Exchange and not directly from St James'.

There was also all the business involving two members of the club board, the chairman and vice chairman, as revealed by a story in the *News of the World*, which had them suggesting that some Tyneside women were dogs and that the fans were being forced to pay a fortune for shirts which only cost a fiver to produce. Little surprise that this caused anger and astonishment among the Toon faithful.

It is funny that Kenny had stuck by the board over the newspaper revelations, we all had, and yet he was sacked as manager. Basically, I think it was a bad time for the club. It was turning into one of the lower periods of my time here.

Once again, the rumours began as to who would be the next manager on Tyneside. Bobby Robson's name was mentioned again, along with a certain Dutchman, and we all know in which order they both came. It was the same old names, with the possible addition of Martin O'Neill, who I believe had his admirers in the boardroom. We soon knew that Ruud Gullit was to be the new gaffer, but I for one couldn't have guessed what times lay ahead. I was to be unwanted and without a squad number over the coming months before the board finally ended Gullit's reign, and my nightmare, almost exactly a year later.

CHAPTER TEN

THE BEST IN BLACK AND WHITE

My choice as the best eleven I have played with during my time at St James' will cause much controversy, I'm sure. A number of players who I think of as friends will be a little upset, but I can assure them that this is the most difficult task of all.

I have selected seven players bought by Kevin Keegan, two by Kenny Dalglish and one by Ruud Gullit; the other, Steve Howey, joined the club from school. So you can gather from this that I believe the side which took us so close to the title in 1995/96 was certainly the most exciting I have played in.

My team is a very fluid 5–3–2 or 4–4–2: Hislop, Dyer, Howey, Venison, Pearce, Batty, Beardsley,

Speed, Ginola, Ferdinand and Shearer. My subs would include Beresford, Albert, Asprilla, Barton and any of three keepers.

Shaka Hislop, now at West Ham United, is my clear choice as goalkeeper. Although he only played 53 league games for the club in his three-year stay, Shaka was, in my opinion at least, a very underrated keeper who never got the opportunities he deserved here. When Kevin signed him from Reading for £1.75 million he came to us with a reputation as being great on crosses and a shot-stopper who commanded his penalty area.

During his time here Shaka proved this to be the case. For some reason though, he was never as popular with the fans as our Czech Republic keeper Pavel Srnicek even though I thought Shaka was the better all-round keeper.

In the end I think Shaka became sick of having to battle to get in the first team every game, and when he was dropped by Kenny Dalglish because he wouldn't sign a new deal he decided to sit it out and move on a free transfer. It was West Ham's gain and our loss as he has gone on to become a very popular member of Harry Redknapp's side.

With three at the back able to play as a unit, I would select Kieron Dyer as my right wing-back. Although he is still only 21, Kieron has the ability to play top-level football for the next decade at least.

He is such a jack in the box and so enthusiastic and energetic in his play but he is one of the worst trainers I have ever seen.

When Keegan was at the club we used to have the tradition of the yellow jersey, which was worn by the worst trainer of the previous session. It really smelt and it had never been washed. On the back it had written, 'I've had a Killer', in honour of Brian Kilcline, who always used to end up wearing it. Sadly, we don't have it anymore, but if we did I'm sure it would say, 'I've had a Dyer.'

Kieron has proven to be Ruud Gullit's best buy during his time at the club, as the former Ipswich Town star has given us so many new options. He can play in any number of positions, down the left, the right or through the middle.

When he gets going with the ball at his feet, he is capable of some wonderful moments of skill which can turn a game on its head. For instance, his superb solo goal against Everton in 1999/2000 was something only he could have produced. Once he learns how to time those surging runs, he will only add to his fast growing reputation. And when he scores more consistently the lads will stop calling him 'Jigsaw'.

I have selected Barry Venison as my sweeper behind the two centre-halves, and I have no doubt at all he would do a great job for me. One of the best-ever value-for-money signings, Venners produced some wonderfully consistent form while on Tyneside. Not bad for a lad brought up to be a Sunderland fan!

No-one wants to win like he does. Off the field you wouldn't find a more relaxed character, but on it he was like a man possessed. Not afraid to tell his team-mates exactly what they were doing wrong, Barry was an inspirational character for us. He loved nothing more than to go out and have a drink, and he was great for team spirit. What's more, he was a superb leader.

I'm glad to see him doing so well for himself off the field working on television as a pundit and presenter. Barry is a bright guy who knows what he wants. But on the field you could never fool him. He always gave his all, every ounce of effort and commitment for the cause, and I know the fans loved him for this attitude.

Many thought his selection for England in 1995 was a huge mistake and yet he proved everyone wrong with a couple of fine shows in a midfield holding role for his country.

When Keegan sold him, he trebled what he paid for Venners, but even then we were all disappointed to see this popular character leave.

Steve Howey must be one of the unluckiest players ever to play for club and country, and surely without the number of injuries he has incurred he would have played many more times for both. After joining the Magpies from school back in 1986 Steve initially made his name as a young striker, but Kevin Keegan initiated a move back into defence which would reap him many rewards.

It came as no surprise when England coach Terry Venables picked out his qualities to select him for England back in 1995. He has the height, the build, pace and determination to play at the top for many more years and it will be interesting to see where his career takes him. But one thing is certain, Steve has a lot of time to make up after such terrible luck, to show that he still possesses all of the attributes which made him such a fine central defender. It was a disappointment when he left the club to join Manchester City in a £2 million deal.

He's a great bloke, Steve, but I'm sure he'll be the first to admit that he's not the brightest. The best example of this was when he made a total prat of himself in front of the manager when KK was in charge. Because Kevin was such a great manager, he wasn't only there for the players if there was a footballing problem, he was everything from an agony aunt to an information service. One day Steve went to see him about something.

'I'm sorry to bother you gaffer, but I've got a bit of a problem at my house. These people have come round to fit a carpet but they've put the wrong colour down. I was wondering if you could have a word with them.'

'Ok,' Kevin said, 'Give me the details and I'll given them a call.'

About half an hour later he's back in touch with Steve. 'I've called them now Steve, but I'm a bit confused. What carpet did you order?'

'Wedgwood,' said Steve.

'So what have they put down then?'

'Blue.'

'That's right then,' said Kevin, 'you ordered Wedgwood blue.'

'No, no,' insisted Steve. 'Wedg WOOD. Wood's brown isn't it. I wanted a brown carpet.'

'Steve, you ordered Wedgwood blue and that's what you've got. I'm not sure I can help you on this one.'

Anyway, in the end Kevin rang the carpet company again and I think he managed to persuade them to fit a brown carpet at half price. I think the moral there is, if you ever come across a carpet company called Howey & Son, steer well clear!

Alongside Steve I have selected Stuart Pearce, if not for his selection of pre-match dressing room entertainment! However, as a player I have nothing but the highest regard for Pearcey. He's a great footballer, with a fantastic temperament and will to win, and with a heart the size of the pitch itself.

In many people's opinion, Pearcey had reached his sell-by date when Kenny signed him on a free in

July 1997, but this could not have been further from the truth. He produced a number of superb performances in the centre of our defence, and anyway, who is going to tell Stuart to his face that he's finished!

Absolutely brilliant in the dressing room and around the club, I believe his treatment from Ruud Gullit was very poor. And, as he has shown at West Ham, he still has so much to offer the game. A player who never accepted the word defeat, Pearcey was a great team-mate and hugely steadying influence on us all.

For Christmas 1998, instead of the usual fancy dress or trip up the Tyne, Pearcey came up with the idea of each player putting their name into a hat, and whoever you drew out you had to buy them a present which was relevant to how they were perceived at the club. All the presents were put in a big tub and handed out and, of course, no-one knew who had sent them. Pearcey got a Zimmer frame – can't think why!, Pistone got a sheep's heart from the butchers, and our German international, Didi Hamann got a copy of Hitler's *Mein Kampf*.

The best one of all though, which unfortunately didn't come off, was Duncan Ferguson. He drew out Nobby Solano, and Dunc tried his nuts off to get hold of a real life llama! He scoured Newcastle for days trying to get one but never did. Just as well really, the gifts were handed out at Austin's, the restaurant next to our Chester-Le-Street training complex – I'm not sure what the members would have made of a llama coming into the bar!

There were a few misleading reports at the time saying some of the foreign players were a bit pissed off with their presents, but to be fair they really got into the spirit of it and took it really well. I got given a £20 note off Didi Hamann because I've got this, totally unjust, reputation for being a bit tight. But to be fair I did put the money straight back into the whip fund on this occasion!

David Batty is a certain selection, no-one could possibly do a better job in that role as the holding player in midfield, or the enforcer, if you want to call him that! But many people seem to forget that David could also play a bit. Under Keegan, after his move from Blackburn Rovers, he was a revelation and so consistent. No-one gave more for the side than Batts did. Under Kenny it was the same, Batts continued to produce any number of superb performances. As with England he never let us down.

But when he became aware that his hometown club Leeds United wanted to re-sign him, there was little if any chance of us holding onto him, as it eventually proved. Batts was hugely grateful to Ruud Gullit for allowing him to move back 90 miles down the A1. To this day, Batts has nothing but praise for our former boss.

An immensely strong, determined footballer who wouldn't take any crap from anyone, Batts was also a hugely likeable guy off the field too. Something few people would believe possible until they are taken into his trust.

Gary Speed is another player who rarely gets the recognition he deserves. And yet every successful side needs a player with his qualities and determination to do the simple things well and leave the other players to pick up the headlines.

During the 1999/2000 season he scored 13 goals from midfield – an amazing tally for anyone, and the best-ever tally for Gary in one season. After a slow start at the club he has gone from strength to strength and I know that all three managers for whom he has played here considered him to be an important member of the side.

With the ability to play either out wide on the left or in a more central role I am certain he would have been a great foil for Batts. Gary's ability in the air is well known, but he also has a good shot on him and when the going gets tough you certainly will not see him hiding at all. The added experience of having captained both his country and former club Everton can have done nothing but good for a player who prefers to keep out of the limelight.

Unsurprisingly, my choice of the most talented player I have played alongside at club level makes the side, and yet his selection will not go down too well with a fair sized proportion of the Newcastle support.

David Ginola arrived at Newcastle in the summer of 1995 to a huge welcome from the Toon Army. Costing the club just £2.5 million, he was an amazing bargain, but he left with a whimper two years later after attacking both the region and the club – something the fans simply will never forgive him for.

There's no doubt in my mind his performances in his first season were some of the best ever produced by a St James' winger. David was simply irresistible, but things began to go wrong from the moment he was refused a move to Barcelona.

However, for all of those problems during his latter days at the club, I will never forget his brilliance. In training he could do things I could only dream about, but he could also leave you frustrated. In my opinion he was the very best I've worked with on sheer talent and quality. And I don't say that lightly. It was always going to be a difficult decision, when you look at the quality of player I have put him ahead of – Alan Shearer, Les Ferdinand, Tino Asprilla, Peter Beardsley, Andy Cole. It really is a difficult choice, but I think our flying Frenchman just shades it.

In fact, I would include in that all the players I have played with for England at international level as well, that is how highly I rate David. I like David

Beckham and think he is a truly great player – he can produce moments of brilliance which leave you stunned. And how can I forget Gazza! However, I think Ginola gets the nod over these two greats, if only just.

David could dribble, he could cross with his left foot at speed with hardly room between his defender and the byline, and he took corners with his left and right foot which I found amazing. And he could turn both ways, he was quick, his physique was so strong and during those early days, after his arrival, I thought he was outstanding.

His strength is so often forgotten, but I am sure his opposition defenders will back me up when I say that he is very strong. Some would suggest, if that is the case, why did he spend so much time on the ground? The reason is simple. I actually believe he sold so many defenders such great dummies they would sometimes clip him and, because of his momentum, he'd collapse in a heap.

I always knew he had ability. But I thought maybe he wouldn't put in the effort when the going got tough, and I thought I was being proven right early on. Keegan had to pull me aside and tell me in no uncertain terms of David's qualities.

David was a great signing for the club and our fans, but also for his team-mates while he was committed to the cause. He was also a very nice guy who got on with everyone, until his standards fell alarmingly. He had flair and charisma and his willingness to mix and accept the odd practical joke at his own expense did not always come over in the media.

However, before his departure to Spurs after only two years at the club, it is fair to say that a lot of the lads no longer got on as well with him. It was when we were struggling as a side and he wasn't pulling his weight that chinks appeared, but I had no problems with him. People may find that surprising now when they see us going at it hammer and tongs when we face one another these days. But there is no malice.

Perhaps over his two seasons he should have done more for us, but that's the sort of player he is. We didn't mind doing his donkey work for him, because he was unstoppable on his day. He wouldn't be able to do it every week, but he was on fire more often than not – until one night when he was sent off for a spat with Lee Dixon of Arsenal. They had clashed in previous games, Dixon felt David was diving when he was challenging him and when they came together once too often at Highbury, David retaliated and was dismissed. I have never seen a player more distraught as he was led from the pitch.

When he stopped breaking down the left and getting in those superb crosses, the problems started to mount. He began to cut inside more, lose

One of my proudest achievements in football – being captain of Newcastle United.

Above: The proudest moment! Leading the lads out at Wembley to face double-chasing Arsenal in May 1998.

Right: Getting a lift, after scoring the first goal of the 1995/96 campaign against Coventry City.

Below: Come in Number 37! It's 30 August 1999, and I'm cheered onto the field by team-mates and fans alike!

Left: Paul Ince and I celebrate after Alan Shearer puts us 1–0 up in our crucial World Cup qualifier in Poland in May 1997.

Below: My best game for my country ends in me setting up Teddy Sheringham for our second, again in Poland.

Left: Let me go Wrighty! I celebrate with Ian Wright after scoring on my debut for England against Romania.

Right: Being chased by Bulgaria's Ilian Iliev in my penultimate appearance for my country, at Wembley in October 1998.

Celebration time. After scoring for England again, this time at Old Trafford against South Africa in May 1997.

Poser! I'm showing off my new club car.

World Cup '98. Glenn Hoddle and John Gorman discuss their next move with me.

Proud to be English! The National Anthem always made the hairs on the back of my neck stand up.

Newcastle and England's 'two dogs', as Kevin Keegan named us. Pardon me, Kev?

Relaxing after an England training session with Steve McManaman and Dennis Wise.

My two England coaches, Glenn Hoddle and Terry Venables.

King Kenny and defensive coach Mark Lawrenson during a training session.

Wor Bobby! Robson returns to breathe new life into the club for 1999/2000.

The new Abba! Me and my wife Anna along with Alan Shearer and his wife Lainya at a club fancy dress.

Happy family! Holidaying in Barbados with Anna and sons Oliver and Elliot.

With John Beresford and Ruel Fox at the opening of 'Football Football', a theme restaurant in London.

Down and out. We crash out of the 1999/2000 UEFA Cup against Italian giants AC Roma. At least I won Man of the Match in the second leg.

My return is complete … well almost! My headed goal in the 1–2 defeat by Chelsea in the FA Cup semi-final tie in April 2000.

My greatest fan James Ibister, who throughout his tragically short life, supported and boosted me especially when I went through hard times under Gullit.

the ball, and then simply starting walking back to help defend his flank.

However, people should remember him at his best for us. He could score great goals in training with both feet and I think it's a shame we let him have his way and leave, as I think he could still have given a lot more to the club. But he'd decided he wanted to go and in the end it was agreed and he moved on to turn in some great performances for Spurs, and then Aston Villa.

Outsiders might think it's strange that he gets such a hard time now from the fans at St James', especially as they reserve wonderful receptions for former players like Ruel Fox, Les Ferdinand, David Kelly and John Beresford. But you're always going to get that if you slag off the area. If there is one thing supporters don't like up here in the north-east, it's former players and people in general having a go at the region. I can understand their point of view. David got a great welcome when he arrived here from Paris St-Germain, in fact they had to place barriers in the car park to keep those fans back as they mobbed him. But when he left, after being transfer listed in April 1997, he did himself no favours by moaning about the area and the people. It was the wrong thing to do and I believe David will eventually come to accept that.

That was why certain players in the Newcastle side, after his move to London, tended to want to get the first tackle in on him whenever we played Spurs. And yet, he still doesn't seem to have learned his lesson. He continues to come out with silly comments when he plays Newcastle which don't help his cause. He chose the wrong person to try and unsettle when he had a go at Alan, during the match at St James' Park in 1999/2000. If he thought he would do anything other than lift Al to even greater efforts, then he was badly mistaken. To be honest they have clashed in several of our more recent meetings, and Al didn't come off second best, I assure you. I don't see much changing now David has signed for Aston Villa.

Alan and David clearly don't get on any more, but that wasn't always the case. At the start they had a good relationship. This was at a time when the Frenchman was flying but then, when quality crosses started to dry up, Al made his feelings plain. But it's the same for us all, no matter who you are, if the crosses are not coming in then Al wants to know why. He made David aware that he wasn't happy, but possibly David thought he was singling him out.

However, in general, he's possibly the best foreign talent the Premiership has had. He's certainly up there with Peter Schmeichel, Dennis Bergkamp and Jaap Stam – they are four of the best in my opinion.

It is quite a contrast between Ginola and another of my choices, Peter Beardsley.

I remember as if it were only yesterday, and not seven years ago, when an excited Keegan rang me and said, 'We've signed Peter Beardsley.' He cost us £1.3 million from Everton and, after I'd seen him in pre-season training I knew we had got another snip. Some doubted Keegan's wisdom, but they needn't have worried.

After recovering from his first broken cheek-bone, he was brilliant. Andy Cole was getting all the plaudits but he couldn't have succeeded so spectacularly without the hard-working Peter. People thought that because he was close to his 33rd birthday when he joined us, it meant he was over the hill and no longer able to produce moments of magic. But he proved them wrong. Once again he demonstrated that age doesn't mean a thing. A good experienced pro is every bit as important as a good youngster.

Maybe it has been unfair to him that you always seemed to hear people talking about Gary Lineker *and* Peter Beardsley, and then Andy Cole *and* Peter Beardsley – Pedro never seemed to get the starring role in some great partnerships. He's always been known as the less publicised partner, simply because the other players alongside him scored all the goals. However, the reason they scored all the goals was because of Peter.

He always scored great individual goals, and yet he was the most unselfish of players. Very unselfish,

I mean, sometimes you'd shout to him, 'Shoot!' and yet he'd prefer to try and set up a goal for his team-mate. He admitted to getting as much enjoyment out of setting up his team-mates as scoring himself.

In terms of his skills, I would undoubtedly describe him as one of the greats. He had a mesmerising trick, his shuffle, which every defender in the country knew about but none could stop. No-one could stop him when he was in the mood, not even in training.

It was bloody frustrating trying to defend against him. He could also spray the ball some distance around the pitch, especially with his right foot. He just used to ping it and nine times out of ten it would drop on your foot or in your path. He'd be trying it on in games even when he was having a bad time, he certainly wouldn't hide. He'd get the ball and still be trying to do the wonder things, very rarely would he be just content to play the simple pass. At times I'd ask him, 'If you're not playing well, why don't you play the simple ball occasionally?'

He would just smile and reply, 'One of those passes could come off at any time to lead to a goal.' Invariably, he was proved right!

When I was just starting in the game, it must have been back around 1984, I saw him chip Brighton keeper Joe Corrigan from the edge of the penalty box to sew up promotion for the club. I can remember the game because it was KK's farewell League appearance. At the time Kevin said Peter was his heir apparent.

Peter could delicately chip the ball better than anyone I've ever known. He used to do it in training for fun, drawing the keeper off his line and then lifting the ball over his head.

There are certain players that you look at and think, 'God, I'd love to play alongside him,' because he would suit your style, and Peter was one of those. I'm privileged to have been able to. He suited the way I played at that time because of the gaps he left. Teddy Sheringham was, and is, also a very good foil, but Beardsley was the best.

My forward duo of Alan and Les are without doubt the best pair I have seen in tandem during my eight years at Newcastle. They had everything in abundance, especially strength. They would take some holding and I for one wouldn't fancy trying to stop them in training, never mind 90-minute warfare.

Les is an outstanding footballer, brave, fast as lightning, brilliant in the air and able to take any amount of stick without complaint. Who can ever forget that great 5–0 hammering of Manchester United in 1996, certainly not the Sky television audience nor a full house at St James' Park. Les scored some of the most exciting goals I have seen, and those who doubt his first touch, believing he hasn't the skill of a Sheringham or a Yorke should ask those defenders who have tried to take the ball from him.

It was no coincidence that we lost the title to Alex Ferguson's men when Les went off the boil after Christmas. But if you were to ask Alan Shearer who was the player he respects as his best partner at this club, I know who he would answer. I have huge respect for Les, and even now I still believe he could do a great job for us.

He came in during the summer of 1995 and grasped the number nine shirt ... with both feet! And within weeks the £6 million fee that we'd paid Queens Park Rangers looked like chickenfeed. Obviously, Keegan decided he was the man to wear the number nine, and I am certain the boss knew it would give Les a boost.

His partnerships with Peter Beardsley and then Alan Shearer were superb. At his best he could do anything, he could drop off, get the ball, run up the middle. He could beat three players and score. And his ability in the air was of legendary status. He was a huge hero with the fans, even when he reluctantly handed the number nine shirt to the then world's most costly signing. And I think it was a sad, sad day when he left the club for Tottenham.

I don't know whether he got on with Kenny Dalglish or not. But Les Ferdinand could still do a job for Newcastle. I'd always buy him. Les played 90 per cent of his games under Keegan, he was never out injured. I just think Keegan knew how to handle him and boost his confidence.

I know he is 33 now, but age is irrelevant. He's still quick and if he could just get his injuries sorted out he'd still cause hell for defenders. He should have scored many many more goals in his career and was without doubt one of the best players we have had. He got Player of the Year while up here but in the end Kenny had his own ideas about who he wanted to play in his attack. Alan was his number one whereas Keegan always wanted them to play together in his side.

Kenny obviously had different ideas and I think Les was told he wouldn't play every game. When you say that to a player, then it does their confidence no good. However, it cost us. Kenny was unlucky after agreeing to let Les go, because of course it coincided with Alan getting injured. These two things combined proved to be a massive blow to us.

Naturally, I cannot finish without a mention for the current skipper, and newly retired England captain, Alan Shearer. You know what you're going to get from Al every game. He simply doesn't play poorly, or if he does it's on the rarest of occasions. I recall one poor game he had, against Middlesbrough away. He was awful, his free-kicks were going over the bar and his passes were flying everywhere. But he had a hernia problem at the time and the following day he went in for an operation. So we'll excuse him for that bad performance!

If you put the ball in the box enough times he's going to score, full stop. You can rely on him to put the ball in the back of the net, and if you had to put your house on any one player taking an opportunity in a game, then this is the man.

He leads by example, but he does like to have his say if the crosses are not coming in for him. And he'll certainly have it out with a few people if they're not doing it on the pitch. But before the team meeting now, the gaffer will ask Alan if he wants to say anything and he'll always say 'No.' He believes the gaffer says everything you need to hear. But after the game, if he's not happy with certain aspects of our performance, especially crosses and forward service, then he will tell you in no uncertain terms. He is proud to skipper his hometown club and expects the same level of commitment from everyone.

He isn't bothered by stick, but he is aware of those who cannot say a good word about him. And yet he never refuses an interview. He can handle the flak because he's had it throughout his career. And when it comes to criticism from opposing crowds, well, I think he thrives upon it. Just look at what happened at his former club Blackburn Rovers in the FA Cup last season. They had a go and he scored the winner!

I think he expects it everywhere now. They never boo bad players, or so he is always telling me! But I don't think the treatment meted out to him had any bearing on his retirement from international football. No, I'm having none of that. I think he's played international football for ten years and it's taken a lot out of him. He's had some serious injuries and I think he realises that some people go on a bit too long.

Is there any kind of jealousy aimed at him? I've certainly never seen any! The truth maybe is that footballers are more likely to be pissed off with fellow players who they think don't deserve the huge salaries and rewards they get without showing the necessary commitment. But Al deserves all he gets. The pressure is on him to score goals. Every Newcastle fan will look to him first, when the chips are down, and nine times out of ten he repays their faith with a result. A fully fit Alan Shearer will produce a higher average goals return than anyone in the Premiership.

He is a very proud man, and all of his team-mates know what it means to him to bring some silverware back to his hometown club. It hurt him as much as it did the most diehard of Toon Army member, when we failed at the last hurdle in the Premiership, in the 1995/96 season, and then lost two consecutive FA

Cup finals. He could have gone to some of the best clubs in the world, including Manchester United. The fact that he chose his own Newcastle when he was in his prime says just how much he loves the club, and everything it represents.

He still wants it as much for the club as he did when he signed in 1996. I've been here eight years and in that time my determination to win something for those supporters has grown. I'm desperate to win something, and he is exactly the same, even more so because he's a proud Geordie.

And he feels he has got a better chance of achieving club success under Bobby Robson. I think everybody feels this, not just Alan Shearer. I think everybody has got to respect the manager they're playing for. And Al has got a great deal of respect for Bobby Robson. If there's someone in charge who you like and who you want to do well for, I think you'll try that bit harder, especially when the going gets tough. Keegan is the prime example, he was my idol, as was Kenny Dalglish. If you don't really like your boss and you've got no respect for him, you're not going to do as well.

Alan will run through a brick wall for Bobby Robson over these coming years. Let's hope we can provide the ammunition because he is still the best at putting the ball into the back of the net.

Weaknesses, what weaknesses? In my opinion he is the complete centre-forward, even his left foot isn't as bad as Gullit would have us all believe. I am not saying his left foot is like Rivaldo's, but I wouldn't say it is a weakness.

True, he's not going to beat five players, go around the keeper and put one in the top corner every week, but he will still score wonder goals. He has also got probably the hardest side foot I've ever seen. He hits it so hard and puts it basically where he wants, which is an art in itself.

He could certainly go on to be a top-quality manager, although it's something you can never tell for sure. Some great players have been known to become poor, unsuccessful managers, but I believe Al possesses the right temperament for it. And, he's certainly a big enough name to attract the best players, which in this day and age is very important.

Alan doesn't always come across that well in the media but that's not the real Alan at all. He just knows that whatever he says will be twisted by the papers so he chooses to play it straight in front of the cameras. But he's always playing practical jokes, although he doesn't like taking them. We got him back for years of throwing water over everybody with a practical joke that really should have won an award it was so good.

It was late summer 1997, not long after Alan had damaged his ankle in pre-season – an injury that kept him out for eight months. One Saturday night, Alan, with his foot in a cast, Bez and a couple of the other lads were round my house. We happened to be watching 'Noel's House Party'. It was the GOTCHA part of the show, where Noel stitches up a celebrity and then presents them with a little trophy. Anyway, Al comes out with, 'I don't know how they get away with this. I'm too clever for them, they would never catch me out with something like that.'

Now ... Alan should have known better than to say something like that and not think we would make him pay for it. So, the next day I pulled a few of the lads together and we started to set the plans in motion.

Al's birthday was coming up and we had already arranged for the players and their wives to go out for a big meal. We booked a private room at a restaurant in Durham called Bistro 21, although the rest of the place would remain open serving other diners. The plan, which *everyone* was in on including the restaurant staff and Alan's wife, was to pay for Bez's sister and her mate, who Alan had never met, to have a meal on us in the adjoining restaurant. Then, after they'd had a few drinks they were supposed to come into our private room and start pestering Alan for his autograph. It went like a dream.

The first time Al didn't take it too badly. He was set upon by these two silly screaming girls. 'Ooh Alan,' they went, 'can you sign this for my mate?'

'Er, yeah, ok,' he said, and off they went.

Then, ten minutes later, they were in again. 'Oh Alan, I forgot, can you sign this for my other mate?'

It went on like this for about an hour. They were taking photographs and everything. Of course, Alan's getting more and more pissed off. He doesn't mind signing a couple but this was his birthday dinner, being totally ruined by a couple of idiots. Every time they went he was on to us, 'I can't believe this, why do they keep coming in?' And all the players played a blinder. 'I dunno Alan,' we'd say, 'perhaps you'd better have a word with them.'

The next time they came in Alan was a bit rude to them, and Bez's sister said, 'I thought you were nice, you weren't like this when we met you at the club.'

'What are you on about?' replied Al, 'I've never seen you before in my life.'

Then Alan's wife got involved and made a great show of confronting him in front of the whole restaurant about these two women he's supposed to have been seeing behind her back!

Anyway, by now Alan's at boiling point, so the next time they came in he tried to throw a glass of water over them. Unfortunately, he picked up an empty one by mistake. Nothing came out – it was bone dry. So he's just stared into this glass and then had to put it back down on the table, which made him look even more stupid.

We had just started to calm him down when the manager came over to inform him that the girls had reported him for swearing and attempted assault and that he was duty bound to call the police. 'I never touched them,' Al pleaded. 'I didn't swear at them. I haven't done anything.'

Finally, the girls came back in again. 'Alan, there's just one thing we want to say to you.'

'Oh yeah,' he replied, getting up aggressively, 'what's that then?'

'GOTCHA,' they said, and Bez's sister pulled out from behind her back this Oscar-type trophy we'd had specially made.

The whole restaurant fell about – the players, the wives, even the waiters. It was a classic.

Before I leave the subject of Alan Shearer, I must put to bed speculation that he was taking Italian lessons in preparation for a move to Serie A, a couple of years ago. There were stories going round for several years that he was continuing to take Italian lessons, and he didn't seem to be too unhappy to let the rumours continue. To be honest, I think it just made him seem a bit intellectual! In actual fact he couldn't speak a word of Italian, he can't even say 'tagliatelle.'

The story first arose during the time he roomed with the then England skipper David Platt, who was playing for Sampdoria. David was taking Italian lessons and I think it was a little bit of two and two makes five. The media picked up hints and came to the wrong conclusion, but Al didn't mind.

He has never wanted to leave this country, and I believe he never will. With his personality there's no way he could get on in a foreign country. He has got a wicked sense of humour and he likes playing tricks. Cutting people's clothes up and pouring water over reporters and fellow players, I don't think he could get away with that in Italy.

So, these are the men I respected most, and would make up my fantasy Newcastle XI.

However, for every star there are many more who play the bit part but are still so vital to the team and to team spirit.

John Beresford is a prime example. We joined the club at roughly the same time, Bez joining three months before me. And we got on very well from the off. We roomed together from virtually the word go until he left for Southampton. We got on great, and many thought we were almost inseparable.

Our fans showed their appreciation of his efforts when he came on as a sub for the Saints at St James' during the 1999/2000 season. They gave him a standing ovation, chanting his name, before he got some good natured booing every time he touched the ball. I know what that meant to him.

Other players could have gone on to be great players for us, if they had that little bit of luck going for them. I've already mentioned Shaka Hislop, full-back Robbie Elliott is another. I think Robbie would have been a good player for us for years. It was unfortunate at the time he left that there were a lot of good players in our squad. He became a little impatient. The same was true of another Geordie, Alan Thompson.

And then there's Darren Huckerby. At the time I didn't think Darren was going to make it to the top. He wasn't totally comfortable with the way we trained. His close skills needed working on to control the ball in our five-a-sides and he often needed two touches. Don't get me wrong, Darren was a good lad, and on the full sized pitch we could all see he was lightning quick, as he showed in a Cup-tie against Chelsea.

He was outstanding in that game after coming on as a substitute. But we never saw that in training. So, when we were offered a million quid for him, I think Kevin was right to accept Coventry's bid. Of course, we didn't have a reserve side so he was not getting games nor the opportunity to impress and improve. But there was no doubt he had frightening pace and I'm pleased he's done well for himself with a good move to Leeds United.

Central defence has always been an area where we've had a number of players to pick from. However, there's no doubt in my mind that the best ball-playing centre-half we've had in my time by quite a long way was Belgian international Philippe Albert.

But one of the most important players in Newcastle's more recent history was Brian Kilcline. 'Killer' was such a nice fella. He was great for team spirit, and even when he wasn't playing he was superb in the dressing room. He was instrumental in keeping the side in the old Second Division, he helped KK in pulling the team around at the last minute.

I'm happy to have to say that I feel I've had a good relationship with almost everyone during my time at Newcastle. Although players are always going to have the occasional spat, especially fiery players, there's been no-one I've disliked. There might be a few players who privately dislike me, I don't know.

There were players who cared so desperately for the club. Lee Clark is an example of this. He would sometimes blow a fuse and I don't think there is any player at the club who didn't have a run-in with him at some stage, but it would soon be forgotten. Nash, a nickname given to him by Terry McDermott because of his resemblance to Dennis The Menace's dog, is a bloke I get on well with, and he is great company.

However, he met his match one day in the huge form of then keeper Pavel Srnicek, a former Czech soldier. Before I arrived at the club, in their fight for survival to stay in the old Second Division, Keegan decided to play his more experienced players, leaving Nash kicking his heels on the bench. Nash, as you can imagine, was not very happy with this. He saw his chance to make his point to the manager in a training match and scythed Keegan down with a lunging challenge.

On seeing this, our Czech 'karate expert' rushed out of his goal and in one movement of his leg, karate-kicked above the height of Nash's head, narrowly missing knocking his block off. It is the only time I have ever seen Nash go quiet! He used to have 'handbags' with everyone in training, but everyone loved him. He wanted so much to play for his hometown club and people understood his frustration when he wasn't selected.

I think we had a great batch of young kids back then. At that stage we were not far behind Man United. We had Steve Watson, Steve Howey, as well as Alan Thompson, Robbie Elliott and Lee Clark. Unfortunately I think that was the last great batch of kids we have had.

And it is funny that the majority have now left the club and had mixed fortunes. I think Thommo's done very well. But someone like Steve Watson has found it tough, as he wanted to play for only one club. I think we needed to keep those players, like Manchester United have done with many of their youngsters. Sometimes the local kids don't get the same treatment as the big signings coming in, so maybe impatience took over.

There is so much more money in the game nowadays. And on top of such huge salaries, a lot of players get sponsorship money as well. People say that all this money and other business interests must distract players from the game, but that's certainly not true in my case. Once I am on the football field, playing football is the only thing on my mind. Sadly, though, there are players for whom money is the be all and end all. So much so that they don't really care if they're playing or not. They still get the same amount of money but they haven't got the pressure of performing every week.

But they're the exception to the rule. And to criticise players who give their all for the club, just because they earn a high salary is just jealousy, pure and simple. No-one really pays too much attention to the tabloids, but players are quickly told if there's a comment about them! Your team-mates will come in for training and give you stick about it, so there's no way of avoiding it.

With the media, it's like anything in life, some people don't get on. If there's a person you're writing about, and you don't really like them anyway, you're not going to give them too much space if they suddenly do well. Some journalists stay quiet when players they don't rate do well, they don't say a word. But then, as soon as the player starts playing badly they start chirping up again. I think you find that with Alan Shearer. When he's having a bad time you see a load of people in the press saying he's past it, but as soon as he starts scoring they move on to another target. At least during the bad times with Gullit, Alan felt the north-east press knew the situation and stood by him.

I do think, however, that newspapers have a great deal of influence, power if you like. At certain times Ruud wouldn't allow the press within 100 yards of the training ground, not realising that he needed them. In fact, he did the same to them as he did to me – kept us both out of sight!

I think the press have got to show the players a certain respect. No player, no matter how big he is, or how much he says it doesn't affect him, wants to see someone slag him off in the papers. We've all had it, we'll all continue to get it, but sometimes it's unnecessary.

CHAPTER ELEVEN

RUUD AWAKENINGS

Contrary to what everyone now believes, I suppose with plenty of reason, my relationship with new manager Ruud Gullit started well enough, and there was no hint that within a few months relations would have deteriorated so much that we would not even acknowledge one another, never mind speak civilly.

At first he seemed to want to talk to his then captain and he was more than happy to take me into his inner circle of advisers and at this stage we had what you might call a relationship of sorts. On his very first day he called the senior players myself, Alan, John Barnes and Stuart Pearce into his office – ironically later the four players he wanted out of the club most – to discuss what went wrong under Kenny. He came across as being very open and a manager you could approach – how wrong could I be!

He would also speak to me as captain on a one-to-one basis, we would talk about things ranging from players to tactics. Of course, I had previously heard rumours that he was arrogant and aloof from what I had read in the papers and from players. But at the time you take people as you find them and at this time I had no problem with him at all.

However, gradually a common subject would be brought up by him in our chats. After a while he began to say to me, 'What's wrong with Alan? You know, I don't think he wants to stay here.'

Gullit was a lot of things, but one thing he certainly wasn't was daft! He knew that whatever he said to me about Alan I, being his best friend, would pass on. Alan from very early on wasn't sure about Ruud and I think he formed a negative opinion of him well before I did. In the end I was becoming a bit of a piggy in the middle, relaying messages from one to the other.

I never really look back to try and bisect what sort of person Gullit really is, but at that time I just thought maybe he was unsure what Al wanted to do. Although Alan never gave any indication at all that he wanted to leave – because it wasn't the case!

Why didn't Gullit go straight to the man himself

and ask him whether he was happy with his lot rather than passing messages through me? He had a couple of meetings with him, but I think because he knew that I was Alan's best mate he preferred to use me as a sort of go-between.

I remember telling Gullit at the time, 'Ask Alan yourself, I mean, that's the easiest thing to do.' I think they are both very strong characters and both are stubborn when they want to be. Both had their own views about why things were not going right with the team.

Gradually, my opinion of Gullit began to go downhill. Not long after he joined, Alan, Dave Batty, and some of the other lads went away on England duty to play against Luxembourg. I was sitting in Batts' room when a call came through from a reporter, saying that a list had been circulated of the players Ruud wanted to put up for transfer. Apparently, myself and Batts were on it. Moments later I got a call, this time from another journalist, saying exactly the same thing.

I wasn't sure what to think but when I got back to the club I confronted Gullit about it. 'I hear you've put out a list with some names of players you want to transfer. I want to know if I'm on it.'

I didn't really mind the fact that I might not be in his plans. After all, he was the new manager, he could buy and sell who he liked. I just wanted him to tell me to my face if he wanted me out.

He stated categorically that I wasn't on the list, and I wasn't for sale, in fact when we then went out for training he started making a joke about it with Steve Clarke. 'Hey Clarkey,' he shouted, 'Rob Lee thinks he's up for sale.'

So I assumed all was well, and yet within months, having made very few first team appearances, I was training with the reserves.

One of the first effects of the new manager was the impact he had on John 'Digger' Barnes and Stuart Pearce. Digger was never involved with the first team no matter how well the ex-England international played in training (and let me tell you that for two weeks he was awesome!) But in Gullit's eyes Digger's legs had gone. Stuart Pearce was slightly different as he played in some early games but I believe this was only because of injuries to other players. Pearcey always gave his all and this was to be his downfall. Unfortunately he was sent off in our home game against West Ham and he never again played for the first team.

Once excluded from the first team squad Ruud hardly ever spoke to, or acknowledged, these two England stars. And that's when I started to think maybe everything was not as rosy as it first seemed. After all, these two hugely respected senior pros deserved better than such disrespect from the manager.

I presume Alan had heard the rumours like the rest of us that Gullit never fancied him as a top class striker, a belief which went back a few years before they met on Tyneside. I honestly can't remember what our reaction was when we were told by Douglas Hall that Ruud was the man to replace Kenny Dalglish. It just happened so quickly. We were just told he was coming and there were quite a few of us who had not met him before.

I have often wondered whether Alan's deep and trusted relationship with Kenny and my publicised feelings for the man had any bearing on Gullit's behaviour towards us. Maybe so, I don't know, but he never raised it as a concern of his. And he was always quick to come out and state exactly what he felt, no matter whose toes he stood upon.

Whatever the truth of the matter, it is no secret that the relationship between Alan and Ruud went downhill pretty early on. A lot of it was played out through the media. Perhaps Ruud wanted him to come out and say something so it brought it to a head. But Alan's very shrewd with the press and he was careful not to have words with the manager on the training pitch as he knew it would get out.

Ruud often accused his players of being selfish, which one or two of us, Alan being one, didn't agree with. But Al never accepted the bait, until he said it once too often. By this stage I had been confined to playing with the reserves and juniors, so I obviously wasn't training with the lads, but apparently Gullit pulled everyone in. I think the results weren't going well and he accused the players of being selfish again. This time Alan spoke up and said, 'Don't call me selfish, because I'm not!'

But despite this, in the early days at least, things in general on the pitch were going okay. At times I felt we played some very good (sexy) football like when we beat Coventry City away 5–1. But in hindsight we were probably just papering over the cracks.

The Board as usual were quick to back their manager in the purchase of Duncan Ferguson for £7 million and we were due to play Everton, ironically on the day he signed. Gullit pulled me before the game and revealed, 'I have made my first signing I have got Duncan Ferguson.' Ruud confided in me first – would you believe it! I was very excited by the prospect of Big Dunc playing alongside Alan Shearer. But had Ruud really bought him to play with Al or to replace him? Only he knows that.

The same day my good friend and midfield partner Dave Batty confided in me that he had asked to leave the club. I was a bit shocked but understood his reasons as the rumours were that his hometown club Leeds United were sniffing around. And it wasn't long before Batts was sold to Leeds for £5 million. Just as disappointingly our long serving Ginger Geordie Steve Watson was sold to Aston Villa for £4 million.

I was having a few problems with my Achilles during this stage of the season and I missed a couple of games. On one occasion Alan was also injured for the game against Wimbledon, Duncan's debut, and we were having bets as to who was going to captain the side. At the time I was a little surprised that he didn't give it to Gary Speed, Alan thought Warren Barton, but we were both wrong! Gullit chose, surprisingly, Steve Howey who was making his comeback after another long absence through injury. Ruud, in my opinion, didn't like many people from the Keegan era but Steve was one of the few.

On the few occasions I had been injured Gullit always seemed to put me straight back into the team until I missed a game at Anfield, on 28 December, that is. I sensed after this that things were beginning to go downhill, and for the next game, against Chelsea, I found myself warming the bench with the now fit Didi Hamann taking my place.

From then on Gullit started his own revolution.

One of his first decisions was to bring in close friend Steve Clarke, who played with him at Stamford Bridge, as his assistant. He also started promoting people from within the club to help him on the coaching side. I believe a lot of people, players and staff alike, were in awe of him because of his massive status within the game. One example of this was when he told his members of staff that pubic hair was unhygienic. One coach, who will remain nameless, immediately went and cut off all his pubic hair! It gave the lads a good laugh!

Following the Chelsea game I was called into the manager's office by Clarke, his messenger boy. Clarke, who stayed on after Gullit's departure until the end of the season, pulled me to one side on the way in and said, 'Whatever Ruud says to you, stay positive, Rob. Keep positive.' I thought it was a very strange thing to say. I should have known what was coming.

I walked in and before I could sit down Ruud enquired, 'How old are you?'

I was taken aback. 'What's that got to do with anything?' I replied.

'I want to know your age,' he persisted.

'I'm 33,' I replied.

And he just said, 'You cannot play in every game – you're too old to play in every game.'

I found his statement amazing, no, insulting! I had played in the majority of his reign at St James' and, I believe, played well. I wasn't going to let it rest.

'Well I am sorry,' I replied. 'I don't agree with you. I haven't been out of the side until before the Leeds game when I got injured, I certainly wasn't playing badly, and then on my return I got man of the match against Leeds. How can I suddenly become too old?'

He countered with, 'You only play for 70 minutes of a game out of every 90.'

To be fair I thought that was quite good!

'No player plays football for 90 minutes,' I said. 'The ball isn't in play for 90 minutes! What the f**k are you talking about?'

Then he said, 'I want to extend your career by playing you in some games, leaving you on the bench in others. And not being involved in others. I did the same to Steve,' looking over at Steve Clarke, 'and managed to extend his playing career to his mid 30s.'

'Well, no disrespect to Steve Clarke,' I replied, 'but I'm an England international and it's certainly not going to extend my England career, more likely it will kill it. I intend playing, I should be allowed to keep playing while I'm performing this well. If I'm not playing well then I can understand you leaving me out.'

He continued to insist, 'I'm trying to extend your career and not shorten it,' and I continued to say, 'You're not extending it, you're basically killing it off.'

Then we started talking about his training methods. I told him, 'Nobody enjoys your training. There's no laughing, there is no team spirit. It is just not enjoyable!'

'You cannot enjoy yourself in training when you are losing games,' he said.

Now, in my opinion, that is totally wrong. I believe just because you are having a laugh and a joke at times in training it doesn't mean you are not working hard.

Anyway, the conversation went back and forth in this manner for about half an hour without us getting anywhere. We agreed to disagree. Of course, this was all very surprising, because only a couple of months earlier he had assured me I wasn't for sale. Now I was being informed I was too old.

Although this constituted a major run in with Gullit, it didn't immediately see me ostracised from the first team squad, but I had certainly lost my starting place during practice matches. Later, I would be switched from the first team to be replaced by young kids. I was used to getting the ball off the back four and turning with it, something I had been doing all my career, but Ruud would shout, 'No! I don't want you doing that, pass it the way you are facing.' And he would replace me with a young reserve.

In my enforced absence from the starting line up Ruud had made Alan, my good friend and Geordie, captain! Because I had been keeping the bench warm all those weeks Gullit had not actually had to confront the question of who was the official team captain, but it didn't take long for the matter to arise. Gullit was forced to bring me back to the starting XI when Gary Speed was suspended for our important home game in the FA Cup quarter-finals with Everton.

I arrived in the dressing room to find I was starting the game. Ruud came in and went through his normal pre-match routine on a flip chart. This is how he had decided to let me know who was captain. I looked at all the names on the chart and next to the name Shearer was 'CAPT'. I couldn't believe it. He didn't even have the decency to tell me to my face! Anyway the meeting ended and Alan stormed off to confront Ruud. He believed like everyone else that when I played I was captain.

Alan caught up with Ruud in his office and asked him what was going on. He was told in no uncertain terms that I wasn't captain, he was, and if he didn't want it he would give it to someone else. Alan said, 'If this is the case then you should tell him to his face!' I don't think Ruud felt he had to explain himself but I was called in by Steve Clarke moments later.

I knew what was coming although it did not make it any easier.

'You are no longer the captain,' he said. 'I want someone as my captain who is behind me 100 per cent! Alan is the new captain and if he won't take it then I will pick someone else.'

I didn't agree with a word he was saying. I certainly never ever gave less than 100 per cent when playing no matter who was manager. But I couldn't be bothered to argue. 'Fine,' I said and walked out.

Maybe Gullit expected Alan to turn it down. And you know, Alan genuinely considered turning the offer of captaincy down. After the Everton game, which we won 4–1 to reach the semi-finals, he rang me up the same evening to ask me. Did I want him to turn the captaincy down? Because if I had a problem with it, he would.

I told him that if I was going to lose it, I would rather lose it to him than to anyone else. I know Alan, being a Geordie, is very proud to captain Newcastle United. And what a great captain he is! But I was gutted when Gullit took it off me. I knew it was coming, but it still didn't soften the blow.

When you have carried the responsibilities of captain with huge pride and tried to represent the club you love with dignity and then it's taken off you, it makes you sick. Gullit didn't even have the guts to tell me first of what he planned to do. I am sure Bobby Robson, Kenny Dalglish or Kevin Keegan would have had the guts to do this – but not the Dutchman.

It was one of the biggest disappointments of my whole career, it was a major blow to me. The honour of the captaincy meant everything to me. I knew it was coming because it was a major topic in press conferences but all Gullit would say was that it wasn't an issue at that moment. He added, 'I'll deal with it when it becomes an issue.' But he never dealt with it, he just dodged it.

I can laugh about it now, when I say to Al, 'I've still got the knives in my back where you stabbed me, you and your mate Ruud,' but at the time it was a real body blow.

But the question remains: did Gullit really want to give the captaincy to Alan or was he just trying to drive a wedge between us? Only Ruud knows the answer.

Gullit was rapidly losing friends and sympathisers at the club – he was even questioning the physios about their treatment methods. Although we were having a surprisingly good run in the FA Cup, in truth the team weren't playing well and a lot of the lads, Alan in particular, were not happy. He got a lot of criticism in the press for appearing miserable, but why should he have walked around with a big smile on his face. He could see the way the club's fortunes were heading. Nobody loves the club more than he does and it really hurt him to see what was happening.

There was no shortage of offers for him from other clubs, but Alan was going nowhere.

If Alan had wanted to go abroad he would have gone. After the Euro 96 championships he had countless clubs after him, Italian, Spanish, London clubs, every club, they all wanted him and he chose his hometown club. It speaks volumes about how much he wanted to play for Newcastle, and he wasn't giving it up as easy as that! But it would have been easy to have thrown in the towel especially as he and the manager didn't exactly see eye-to-eye.

For instance, I recall on one occasion the two were playing a practice match, Ruud on one team Alan on the other, the ball was played into Alan's feet, he swiftly turned with it and powered an unstoppable shot into the top corner with his right foot, the sort of thing he has been doing for years in the Premier League.

A great goal you would think, Ruud didn't think so. He started shouting at the young player marking Alan, 'Keep him on his left foot, you know he hasn't got a left foot'. Nice coming from your manager!

Anyway, the next ball comes into Al's feet, he controls it superbly turns in one swift movement and smashes another shot into the top corner with, yes you've guessed it, his trusty *left* foot. 'Not bad for someone with no left foot Al' shouted our quick-witted keeper Steve Harper.

However, it wasn't only Al who was gunning for Gullit, Stuart Pearce was also looking to rid himself of the frustration he was feeling with a little tomfoolery in training. He asked the lads to make a pass short when he was directly faced by the Dutchman. 'Leave the ball between us,' he said.

Anyway, sure enough the first chance he got he went steaming in and sent Gullit into orbit. Now Gullit's a big bloke and to be fair he took the challenge well, but needless to say he never got involved in a 50:50 challenge with Pearcey again.

Pearcey didn't have a lot to lose. I think Ruud had told him that he would never play another game for the club. And this at a time when we were struggling for centre-halfs and were playing kids there. We were just totally lacking any experience, and I know Stuart, a guy who cares passionately about his football as well as punk music, was becoming so frustrated. I felt he could still have played his part.

Returning to the footballing side of things, after our 4–1 demolition of Everton, I was dropped for the next game. Out went Lee and back in came Speed! Don't get me wrong, Didi Hamann and Gary Speed in particular were playing very well but I still believed I had a lot to offer. It made me laugh when Ruud came out with a statement saying that he had resurrected Gary Speed's Newcastle career. Rubbish! Gary Speed, although by his own admission had a poor start to his career at St James', was playing very well before Ruud turned up. At the start Speedo was, in my opinion, being played out of position on the left wing. Now that he is in the middle of midfield he is proving what a great box to box player he is. In fact he had his best season in goalscoring terms in 1999/2000 with 13 goals.

Over the remaining months of the season I had several meetings with Ruud, and also Freddie Shepherd, to try and resolve my situation. It was during one of those meetings that I saw the real Ruud Gullit, showing his obvious disdain with anything from Newcastle's past. I don't know whether he felt threatened by the Keegan era but he certainly wasn't a fan of it. He said, 'You weren't such a good team. We [Chelsea] used to enjoy coming up here and beating you lot.' Call me picky, but I couldn't remember them actually doing that. Maybe he meant the cup game when they beat us on penalties!

He also said, 'People in London were laughing at you when you blew the title!' What a thing to say about the club you're in charge of!

Despite this latest spat, I managed to keep myself in and out of the team for the rest of the season. But whenever I was named in the side it was out on the right wing, a position I'm sure everyone knows, including Ruud, is not my favourite. Gullit and I hardly spoke during these months and I wasn't expecting to be playing come FA Cup semi-final day against Tottenham at Old Trafford.

I was in the team in my 'favourite' right wing position. My job? To help our full back Andy Griffin with a certain David Ginola. I didn't enjoy many games during Gullit's brief reign, but if I am being honest this was one day I will remember for a long, long time. As I have mentioned I missed the FA Cup semi-final the previous season through injury, so Ruud had in fact given me my first opportunity to play in a semi-final.

The semi went very well for myself and the team with Alan Shearer, who else, scoring twice to give us a 2–0 win and I am sure everybody will remember Gullit's cuddle with Alan after the victory.

We now had an FA Cup final against Manchester United to look forward to. Maybe the season wasn't going to be too bad after all. Mind you, from the semi to the final we never won a single game! Our bad run obviously concerned Gullit because before the game he asked our kit man, Ray Thompson, to sprinkle salt around the dressing room when he was laying out the kit – presumably in an attempt to bring us good luck. Again, I wasn't expecting to be in the starting line up for the final but, to my amazement, I was included, although in my now usual right wing position.

The game was a non event as far as we were concerned, although we did in fact start the game very well until Manchester United had to make an early substitution due to injury. Roy Keane went off – great we thought! But on stepped Teddy Sheringham and within five minutes he had put them one-up. And that is how it stayed until half time.

Ruud wasn't best pleased with a number of performances, I don't know about mine because he never spoke to me! But at half time he decided to replace our Peruvian winger Nolberto Solano with Temuri Ketsbaia. Nobby was understandably very disappointed and started to get undressed ready for a shower when suddenly Didi Hamann announced he was injured and couldn't continue in the second half. Ruud immediately told Nobby to get his kit on again.

In the second half we conceded a second goal via Paul Scholes and the game was over. Again we had come to Wembley and not played at all!

After the game we all went for the customary banquet at our hotel in London to try and drown our sorrows. The players all met up with their families and sat down for an end of season meal. Gullit kept his distance. He had his own table with his friends. He stayed for the meal and then gave an extraordinary speech about how well he had done to get this team to the Cup final. He also said how it was a new experience for him losing as he had never lost a final before.

He then made a quick exit and I believe went to a club in London, returning the next morning to travel back to Newcastle with the team for the already organised bus parade.

Thousands of Geordies again lined the streets of Newcastle to greet their fallen heroes on an awful day. It was pouring with rain and it was an open top bus. Gullit spent the majority of the time reading his paper, he only popped up every so often before disappearing downstairs again. Okay, it was pissing it down but thousands of Geordies had turned up to give us their support and I think he was wrong to not make more of an effort.

The bus tour parade came to an end at the Civic Centre in the city and we all appeared on the balcony to thank the fans. Gullit made a brief speech and then, within ten minutes he was off, in a car to the airport and back to Amsterdam.

The next time I saw Ruud Gullit was for the start of the following season, one which fortunately was to be his last, but what a season it turned out to be for yours truly – my number was up!

CHAPTER TWELVE

NEW HORIZON

Having spent the summer getting over the disappoint-ments of the previous season, I returned from a break with my family in Barbados looking forward to a fresh start. After speaking with a few people who I genuinely respected, Kevin Keegan included who I met while on holiday, I decided I would give it one last go to prove Gullit wrong. I was more determined than ever that I was not going to leave the club I had grown to love and feel part of without a fight!

But I should have known from the first week back my plan of getting my head down, working hard and hopefully forcing my way back into the manager's plans was a non-starter. As the first team squad flew out to Holland and then Scotland for a few pre-season games, I found myself, not on the plane with them as I expected, but training with Tommy Craig and his reserves' squad at our Chester-Le-Street training ground. I was joined by Stuart Pearce who also found himself not part of the manager's plans.

Clearly something was up, but I didn't realise the gravity of the situation until the squad assembled at St James' for the traditional team photo. I went to put my boots on but couldn't find them. I was sponsored by Puma at the time and obviously I wanted to wear their boots, but they had vanished. Gullit tried to make me wear Adidas ones instead. In the end I found some old Puma trainers and decided to put those on, not that it mattered what I wore really because no-one could see them! For the team photo out on the pitch I was stuck right at the back almost out of sight. Out of sight, out of mind?

Back inside, I bumped into the club Press Officer, as was then, Graham Courtney. I told him about the boots and asked if he knew what was going on.

'You haven't got a shirt,' he said.

'Oh right,' I replied, 'you mean I haven't got the number seven.'

'No, you haven't got a shirt at all.'

I couldn't believe it. If I was not going to be in Ruud's first team squad, then fine, I'm a big boy, I can take it, but he could of at least given me a higher squad number. But to not give me any number at all made no sense. I found it funny in some ways. Gullit must have known he would face a backlash from the fans. I'm not being big-headed but I was one of the fans' favourite players. They would have bought their season tickets to come and watch me and the other players perform, and here I was without so much as a shirt on my back!

I can only conclude Gullit was trying to make a point. Alan couldn't believe it when I told him. At first he thought I was pulling his leg, but as I came to realise in the coming months one thing it wasn't, was a joke.

So, it was back to training with the reserves with Tommy Craig. To be fair he was brilliant, he understood the situation I had found myself in, always encouraging, even when I was having a bad day! Those days didn't come too often in the beginning, but once Pearcey had managed to 'escape' to West Ham, they became more frequent. The more the pre-season dragged on the worse it got.

It seemed Ruud didn't want me anywhere near the first team, for days at a time I wouldn't even see them never mind train with them. On the really dark days, I would turn up for training, only for Tommy to reluctantly say to me,

'Sorry Rob, the manager's having a practice match this morning and you're not involved'.

'How many of us are not involved Tom?' I enquired.

'Just you! If you want, you can go and train at Maiden Castle with the kids or if not get yourself off home.' I'm sure he found it as amusing and unbelievable as I did.

So the normal routine was to travel the five miles or so to train with Kenny Warton, Alan Irvine and the academy kids and to be quite honest, I found myself actually enjoying training again, something which I hadn't done for a very long time under Ruud Gullit. It was great to see young lads enjoying learning their trade, they were working hard but they were doing it with a smile on their faces. Smiling faces is certainly something I hadn't seen too much of whilst training with the first team.

Once the season got under way the novelty of training with the kids began to wear off and I found myself on more and more occasions feeling depressed thinking, 'I can't go on like this for ever, less than a year ago I was an England player and now I do not even have a squad number for my club, I am going to have to leave.' That was the last thing I wanted to do, but as time wore on it seemed the only option.

Mind you, in some ways I was well out of it – all was not well in the first team camp. The team had started in the worst possible fashion, a defeat at home to Aston Villa with Alan Shearer being sent off in one of the worst refereeing decisions I'd seen in a long time. Ruud had spent heavily again in the summer recruiting Alain Goma, Marcelino, Kieron Dyer and Franck Dumas but it was taking them time to settle and the results were going from bad to worse.

Defeats away, first at Tottenham and then Southampton, had people asking questions about the manager's position. On the training ground there was also a bit of unrest especially between the manager and his skipper, they seemed to always be at each other's throats. Maybe the fact that Alan had just signed a new five-year contract, which I'm sure Ruud didn't know too much about, had made things worse.

With pressure mounting, the next home game, against Wimbledon, had become a crunch fixture. Surely this was a game that if we won heavily the pressure would be off Ruud. He also had the opportunity, with Alan suspended after his Villa sending off, to show the whole of football Newcastle could do without their centre forward.

The game seemed to be going to plan with us taking a 3–1 lead with five minutes to go and the chants of 'Ruud Gullit, Ruud Gullit' ringing around the ground from the Geordie faithful. I took the opportunity to have a long look round our impressive stadium thinking that maybe Ruud had won and I had, in fact, played my last ever game at St James' Park. But amazingly, within that five-minutes period we conceded two goals to finish drawing 3–3. The singing had stopped and the team left the field to a chorus of boos.

Wednesday 25th August, 1999, that is a date that I, Ruud Gullit and the fans will remember for a long time. It was Sunderland at home, the most important game of any season for Geordies but this one in particular took on even greater significance. Although I didn't play, it was that game, and the aftermath, which indirectly saved my Newcastle career.

Ruud actually spoke to me for the first time in ages on the morning of the match. As he called me over I thought surely he not going to ask me to play against Sunderland, he couldn't, could he?

'Trevor Francis wants you to go to Birmingham,' he said coldly.

'I'll think about it,' I replied.

That was it, the quickest meeting ever!

After training with Tommy and the reserves Steve Clarke approached me. 'Colin Lee wants to take you to Wolves, do you want to speak to him,' he said.

'Look Clarkey,' I retorted, 'you tell Ruud if he wants to get rid of me then get me a free transfer, stop coming to tell me about this club and that club. Sort me out a free and I'll leave, I'll be out of your hair.'

It was a bit of a bluff on my part really, I thought there was no way the board would agree to that, would they?

'OK,' he said, 'let's get tonight's game out of the way and I'll speak to Ruud and see what we can do.'

So, my fate would be decided after the big derby match, but not in the way I thought!

As anticipation for the game grew stronger during the course of the day, rumours spread like wildfire that Alan Shearer would not start the game. Surely it was just a rumour? Gullit couldn't possibly leave out his best player from such an important game could he? But I spoke to a few local newspaper men and they were all telling the same story. They couldn't believe the decisions Gullit was making and the majority of journalists believed he was on his way out and not too disappointed about it either. He was taking on the fans' hero and was clearly losing the propaganda battle.

I think Gullit had reached the stage where he expected the board of directors to either back him or sack him. He dropped the bombshell of leaving Alan out and also not playing Duncan Ferguson who was just returning from injury.

Unfortunately for Ruud, in the north-east, no-one is bigger than Alan Shearer. I think he thought he'd experiment with leaving them out and just see what happened. It might have worked. Maybe if we'd have beaten Sunderland not too much would have been said, I don't know but you surely you don't go into a game against your deadliest rivals, who were flying high in the league, not starting with an international strikeforce worth £23 million.

Though that is what happened. Shearer and Ferguson sat on the bench, while our promising, but still inexperienced, young kid Paul Robinson led the attack.

That night was one of the bleakest and most rainswept nights I can remember during my time at the club.

I wasn't even at the game, I missed my first home game for many a year as I no longer felt welcome by the management, who probably preferred it that way as well. I sat at home flicking through Teletext with a good pal of mine, ex-Durham and England cricketer John Morris. The score came through that Kieron Dyer had put us one up after 28 minutes. I am not proud to say that my heart sank.

For the first time I really thought I was going to have to leave the club I'd come to love, Gullit was getting his way, he felt he had already disposed of me and now what made matters worse, we were beating our arch rivals Sunderland without a certain Alan Shearer in the side – what was Newcastle United coming to?

I couldn't bear to watch it so we turned the Teletext off and watched something else while we drank a glass of red wine. When I turned it back on with about ten minutes to go, fearing the worst, I was astonished to see we were now 2–1 down. Niall Quinn, equalising after 64 minutes, and Kevin Phillips, ten minutes later, had given them the lead! I repeat, I had never before wanted any Newcastle side to lose. Even when I have been out of the side injured I always wanted my club to win without me. Now it was different, so very different.

It was getting to the stage where, maybe, if we lost a couple more of our games then Gullit would surely be out. A good thing for the club as a whole and certainly for me. I wasn't in the least bit disappointed when I heard the final result of that derby clash. I knew our fans would be down, they would be very angry. After leaving both Alan and Duncan Ferguson on the substitutes bench, Gullit had lost his greatest gamble.

I listened to Ruud's post-match comments with utter disbelief, he was actually blaming Alan and Duncan for the result stating that Newcastle weren't losing until he brought the two subs on. There were two rather pissed off players waiting to see Mr. Gullit when he arrived at training the next morning. Al and Big Dunc stormed in one after the other fuming about his comments, wanting an explanation. I don't know what was said in either case but I do know that the manager was losing the support of what few players he had left.

Alan rang me early on the Friday morning to say that Ruud had been sacked although I already had an idea when I picked my morning papers. When I arrived at our training ground later that morning it was confirmed. Steve Clarke, his assistant, broke the 'sad' news to us all.

If Gullit had stayed I would definitely have gone, without a shadow of a doubt. I was days away from going, days away, but only if they'd have granted me a free transfer. I was pretty sure though they wouldn't give me one, the board wouldn't have agreed because through all this time I continued to get on well with the chairman Freddie Shepherd.

However, I knew, to a certain extent, that the board had their hands tied, because they had to be seen to back their manager. Gullit was their choice after all. I understood that. Until it got to the stage where my shirt was taken away, Ruud had made a decision about a player and the Board had to be aware of why. They might not have agreed with it but had to stick with him. The more I look at the situation over him taking my shirt from my back and my squad number, I think it damaged him more than it damaged me. My popularity among the fans seemed to grow as a result.

It saddens me now that Bobby Robson has got so little money to spend and yet Gullit had so much money available. He spent £32.8 million in all.

It's an amazing amount of money but I think when you're going to give a manager that sort of money you've got to keep him on, even if you're having a bad time. I remember when Alex Ferguson first went to Old Trafford they were having a shocker and people were calling for him to get the sack. Their board stuck with him and now look at what has happened.

This was never going to be the case with Ruud after the defeat by Sunderland. It was a bridge too far. Now he had gone perhaps I would finally get a run in the first team that I felt I deserved. Steve Clarke took over the reins in the short-term. He confirmed what everyone already knew on that Friday morning, that Gullit had gone, and moments later he called me in to see him.

He sat me down and said, 'How fit are you?'

'How f**king fit do you think I am?' I replied. 'You have made me train with the kids for the last two months.'

'That was Ruud's decision,' he insisted, 'he wanted you out. Don't you think I was trying to get you back in the team?'

'Were you ?' I asked.

'Of course I was but Ruud had made his mind up and refused to listen to anyone. Look Rob, I'm in charge for the game at Manchester United in two days' time and I want you to play. Do you think you can get through a game? '

'I have no idea how long I'll last,' I said.

'Just last as long as you can, if you can get to 60 minutes that will be great, even 45 will be good.

Anything really, but I want you to start,' Steve replied.

It was ridiculous really. There he was asking to me to play at Old Trafford against the best team in Europe, and I hadn't played a competitive game since July. My head was telling me not to play because I wasn't sure of his motives. But I remember when he met with the press he gave the impression he definitely wanted me back in because he felt I'd strengthen the backbone of the team. Why the hell did Gullit not swallow his pride and realise that too! My heart was telling me that I wanted to be back out there playing, I wanted to be involved even if it was for just 45 minutes.

Steve said, 'Obviously you need a squad number – what number are you after?

'What numbers are there left?' I asked.

'Thirty-three is there, do you want 33?'

Thirty-three was my age at the time so I thought, 'Sod it,' I didn't want that, leaving me open to people making comments about my age. So I thought I'd have 37, at least that had my seven in it.

Come in number 37 !

I think the majority of people were pleased Gullit had gone. There was a new sense of optimism amongst fans and players alike. All of a sudden I had gone from playing with the kids to playing with the first team at Old Trafford of all places. I think the speed of my return even caught the club by surprise because, when we arrived at Old Trafford, I found I had a different shirt from everyone else. Ray Thompson, our kit man, explained he had to go and get a replica shirt from the club shop, my name and number were ironed on and the Newcastle Brown Ale logo was much bigger than everybody else's.

There was also a lovely touch from Kieron Dyer, who I had only just met due to my enforced absence. He offered me my shirt back. I politely declined, thanked him for his offer and told him to wear it with pride, which he certainly did! He is going to be a fantastic player for Newcastle United.

As I ran out onto the pitch the response I got from the Geordies in the crowd was an unforgettable experience. They were singing my name, it was ringing all around the stadium. I don't know how many thousands were there but I got an unbelievable reception, I was even clapped on by a few of the lads as well. It was a great feeling to be back, but I just stood around, did a few stretches and was simply conserving my energy.

It was a very warm day, if I remember right, which didn't help given my lack of fitness. The game wasn't going too badly, my energy levels seemed okay, until I had to chase Ryan Giggs down the wing – they dropped dramatically after that. I managed to get to half time, the score was a respectable 1–1. Not bad I thought. Then, with only moments of the second half played we were 2–1 down and had Nicos Dabizas sent off. A few minutes later we were 3–1 down. Exit Rob Lee from the field of play, knackered. The final result was a crushing 5–1 defeat. Welcome back!

That was Steve Clarke's first and only game in charge. By the end of the next week we had a new manager – Bobby Robson. I had read the papers, like everybody else, so I knew Bobby was in the frame but I had no inside information. He was officially unveiled on 2 September, 1999 – the Thursday before the away game at Chelsea. There was hardly any time at all for him to do anything to influence the match at Stamford Bridge.

The first I saw of him was when he came down to the training ground to meet us. I knew Bobby was from the area and clearly had a love of the football club. It was a welcome change to have someone from the north-east who had an affinity with the people and the place. That was certainly something we lacked with the previous manager.

It was little more than a quick introduction, shaking hands with all the players. Then he took a quick training session before we travelled down to London to face Chelsea – it was all go. But already Bobby's enthusiasm was shining through and giving the lads a lift. I think the thing you notice about him, even when he was doing his first session, was his enthusiasm – 'Get the ball, get it son,' he'd encourage. He was doing all the actions and this, allied to his enthusiasm, just rubbed off on everybody. A big cloud was lifting from the club, even though we were bottom of the league with just one point from six games.

The team was announced on the Friday, before he went through a few things. It was his team from the start, although I think he must have watched the Manchester United game on video to get a better idea of the players. The only thing I was looking at was whether I was in it, luckily enough I was.

After our meal on the Friday evening myself, Alan and Duncan were called to see Bobby in his hotel room. He was in the penthouse suite right at the top of the hotel – Bobby couldn't find his way around it at first, it was such a big place. He had a brief chat with both me and Duncan, for different reasons we hadn't played many games; Duncan had been injured, a long term injury, while I'd obviously been out for other reasons.

'Now lads,' he said, 'I know you've missed a lot of training and haven't played many games but the more games you play the fitter you will get.' He said he wanted us both to start against Chelsea which was great to hear.

Alan stayed behind when me and Duncan left and had a chat with Bobby about what had happened and how he thought he could improve

Alan's game. This was music to Al's ears I'm sure, his manager taking a big interest in him again. Alan and Bobby got on very well from the word go, they have a mutual respect, something which was lacking with Gullit.

Bobby changed the system straight away against Chelsea, playing Warren Barton on Gianfranco Zola while Nicos Dabizas played as a sweeper. It worked very well and they only beat us by a dubious penalty. Chelsea were in the top two at the time and we were at the bottom. However, we'd gone there and certainly not been outplayed. Gianluca Vialli was very generous in his praise for us after the match, his respect for the new gaffer was clear to see.

Although we were bottom of the table we had a lot of games to play so we knew there was something to build upon, it wasn't like we had two or three games left at the end of the season and performances didn't matter. We needed to get our performances right, and people playing with confidence.

As the confidence grew so training became fun again, and the music was back in the dressing room. We used to play music in the dressing room before games under Kenny, Stuart Pearce used to bring his tapes in, which was an acquired taste to say the least, Sex Pistols, Squeeze and some I have never even heard of but we enjoyed it all the same.

I'm not sure Bobby is a punk rock fan – I think he likes Chris de Burgh – but he didn't mind at all. Most importantly the fun was back and not a moment too soon.

And then, on 19 September came the visit of Sheffield Wednesday, a brilliant 8–0 victory. It was amazing, because the early part of the game was dominated by them. In the first ten minutes they played very well and we were hanging on but the turning point was when Andy Booth, their big centre forward, got injured and had to leave the field.

We had been under a bit of pressure but once Aaron Hughes scored with a header, it gave us a huge lift – you've got to remember we were bottom of the league and they were just above us. We went into overdrive and it was plain sailing from then on really. Every time we took a shot at goal we scored, it was just one of those days. I mean, we'd had a few big wins in the past but this was something else. This in Bobby's first home game too.

In the dressing room afterwards we were full of ourselves. I think Bobby did his best to calm us down, but it's difficult to keep a team down when they've just won 8–0 at home. Even Manchester United, who were the best team in Europe, weren't doing that to too many people.

On a personal level, it was the first game in which I played a full 90 minutes. I was pleased to get that under my belt, I'd come from 55 to 70 to a full 90 now, I was feeling fitter and stronger every game.

Bobby was also settling down very quickly, his enthusiasm and humour brought smiling faces all around the ground. You can have a good laugh and a joke with him as well. He has a reputation in football for getting players' names wrong. There's the famous story about him when he was the manager of England. He passed Bryan Robson one morning on the way down to breakfast. 'Morning Bobby,' he said.

The England skipper had to correct him. 'No boss, you're Bobby, I'm Bryan.'

Since he's been at Newcastle he's forever calling Kieron Dyer, Kevin. He also gets a bit confused in team talks. He'll say something like, 'Now lads, make sure you all pass to Warren more today.' Then someone will pipe up, 'But boss, Warren's not here today.'

Mind you, half the time I'm sure he does this on purpose, to get the lads going and have a bit of a laugh. If he does get something wrong he'll make a joke about it, 'Well, what do you expect from someone who is 68 now?'

There is also a very tough side to the manager too and when he's angry everyone knows about it in the dressing room. For instance he blew his top when we played Liverpool, at Anfield on 25 March, 2000 and conceded a goal in the last minute scored by Jamie Redknapp. He was very, very angry because he'd seen how hard we'd worked and how we'd clawed ourselves back from defeat – we didn't play well but we'd stopped Liverpool playing.

His anger was a general thing. He directed it at everybody throughout the team, he believed our team defending cost us that last minute goal. He started, 'Warren you shouldn't have lost the ball, and Nicos you shouldn't have booted it out for a corner, and Didier you should have marked him when the cross came in from the right,' and … he went through the whole team. He wasn't happy!

In general those battling performances at Stamford Bridge, Anfield and also Highbury, where we got a point, epitomised the new togetherness, I believe brought about by Bobby's great man-management and his ideas of how we should stick together off the field.

For instance we have to go for lunch together at the training ground, if anyone is late or doesn't turn up then they are fined. We all leave at the same time and Bobby is much stricter with anyone who is late for training. There are no exceptions. The fine for being late is a fiver, doesn't sound much does it? Let me tell you though players hate having to pay it. As they say, it's the money not the principle!

Warren Barton, our entertainments manager, collects all fines with the proceeds going into a pot for all the lads to enjoy a night out. Now there are some players who are very generous with their donations to the 'pot', Kieron, who we call 'Pin Head' because of his really small head, is one of those. He is always late no matter how many times you tell him or how much you put the fine up. Mind you, he is a prompt payer unlike some I could mention – with Steve Harper it's like getting blood from a stone! But you can always rely on Pin Head.

I think it's almost compulsory if you're a professional footballer to have a nickname. John Barnes was always 'Digger' because of the character in the 1980s TV series *Dallas*. I've had a couple over the years as well. When I was at Charlton I was always called 'Lurker' because people said I'd been lurking about south-east London for years. That stuck when I came up to Newcastle, until we were on a pre-season tour to China one year under Keegan. We had just signed Al from Blackburn Rovers and the side was littered with top-quality flair players. We were about to play the Chinese national team and in the team meeting beforehand, with the likes of Les, Tino, Peter and David Ginola all sitting around, Kevin said, 'Don't forget all you players, don't abuse my two dogs in midfield,' – referring to me and Dave Batty. From then on it stuck. I'm always called Dog or Doggy now.

Bobby has also introduced fines for leaving on mobile phones during team meetings or on the team bus. I remember we were playing Wimbledon away last season. When we came in at half time I reached into Alan's pocket and switched on his phone. Then I disappeared off to the toilet to call him on it. I came back in the middle of Bobby's half time team talk with Alan's phone ringing. 'Who's mobile is that?' I asked in all innocence. Bobby tried to hit him with a hefty fine but Al wasn't having it claiming it was a set-up. I still don't think he knows who did it. He will now.

Bobby continued to build on the decent start we had under him. He must have been told when he took the job that there wouldn't be much money to buy players so what he did have, he had to spend very wisely. Kevin Gallacher was his only major buy in the 1999/2000 season, but in my opinion he has proved to be great value at £500,000, playing in a number of different positions, running his heart out and also chipping in with some vital goals.

Bobby also added to his back room staff, bringing in the ex-Carlisle, Scarborough and Colchester manager Mick Wadsworth to be his first team coach and Gordon Milne as General Manager. Both people he knew well and trusted to help him in what is a massive job.

By December 1999 things were looking better, we had managed to claw ourselves up into about 14th position in the table, no mean feat considering we had one point from a possible 21 at the start. My own personal form was also very good, I even had calls for me to be reinstated to the England squad, something I knew would never happen, but it was nice to prove a few people wrong who doubted I could still be a force in the Premier League. Take note Mr. Gullit!

I never lost faith in my ability. I always maintained, and still do, that Newcastle are a better team with me in the side. I hope that doesn't sound big-headed, because I'm certainly not, I just believe I can still perform at the highest level.

Back in the team and playing with confidence I decided to sit down with Bobby to ask him if I could come off the transfer list which I had been put on months before.

He was shocked. 'What, you're on the transfer list?' he said.

'Yes I am, I've been on it since Ruud was here.'

'Unbelievable,' he said. 'Don't worry I'll make a statement and say you're definitely off it.'

I said, 'Look, if I'm not part of your long term plans, then fine, leave me on it.'

He assured me that I was and that he would come out in the press and make a statement to that effect, which he did. He made me feel wanted again.

Bobby has also invested money in the future of the club by signing young players with bags of potential such as Paraguayan international Diego

Gavilan. Bobby has had him watched numerous times and kept tracking the player even when it looked unlikely he would be able to find the cash to secure his signature. I haven't seen too much of him so it's difficult to judge him but I trust the manager's judgement. Diego's over here with his mum and dad, which is good for him. I don't think you're going to see the best of him for at least a year or so.

I believe this club has come so far since I signed nine years ago and I am confident it is now too big to fall back to the bad old days. I believe we have come through a few of bad years and we are now ready – if the manager is given some cash to spend – to get the club back into the upper regions of the Premiership.

I think football's gone crazy since I joined this club. Football in general has gone very high profile, players are like pop stars now, when I started they certainly weren't and the game was very close to disappearing as the national sport. Just look at Charlton, we were getting 4,000 fans regularly, but now they're getting 20,000 sell-outs every week. Back in the mid-eighties most clubs, not even Man United, were filling their stadiums. I think a lot of them were going backwards until BSkyB came in and made the game into a viable entertainment.

The sport has gone from being a game to a major industry and I think people take it a bit too seriously now. I still like a laugh and a joke. Don't get me wrong when I pull on the Newcastle shirt I give 110 per cent but there's got to be room for some fun. It is a sport after all. It's sad in a way that it's become much more of a business but I guess it all comes down to money at the end of the day.

The Newcastle fans deserve success. They follow us in their thousands, a lot of them even come to the training ground. In fact it got to an unbelievable level in the 1990s at our old training ground in Durham. They would all crowd round the edge of the pitch, about 50 deep. It was like the 1923 FA Cup final at Wembley, when a lone policeman on a white horse fought to hold back the crowds after they spilled onto the pitch. After a while the amount of fans was so huge that enterprising hot dogs sellers and ice cream vans started coming down, to cater for the hungry thousands. Keegan never used to let us forget that we had to show our appreciation. After training, even if it was freezing cold, he would make sure we stayed to sign every last autograph.

If there is one thing I have learned during the latter years of my football career it is you must always show your supporters respect and appreciate them. Hopefully I do that.

Since I've regained my place in the team under Bobby, after such a long, enforced, absence, it has made me appreciate the playing years I have got left all the more. I want to carry on playing for as long as Newcastle will have me – hopefully a couple more seasons at least. When I do finally call it a day I'm not sure what I'll do. I'm doing a coaching badge at the moment and that is something I could certainly see myself moving into, but there's a long way to go yet.

I know a lot of Geordies have speculated about me teaming up with a certain Alan Shearer in the not too distant future, to become joint managers at St James'. Of course, it's all just rumour, but I'd welcome the chance to stay on at the club in some capacity, and then who knows? I'm a strong believer in fate, and I'm sure I'll end up doing what's right for me, so I wouldn't rule anything out!

Number 37's time was up, but only because I was given my old number seven shirt back at the start of Bobby's first full season in control. Two months later I signed a new deal with the club and was back playing and enjoying my football as much as ever.

CHAPTER 13

ANNUS HORRIBILIS

Season 2000/01 amounted to nothing short of annus horribilis as far as my ninth season at St James' Park was concerned. Why had so much promise been dissipated into a time of under-achievement and almost constant stress with injuries dogging many of our key players?

It began with injury to Alan Shearer and his new strike partner Carl Cort, and ended with Al flying out to America to see the world's top knee specialist. Al has had a number of operations, whereas my operation at a local hospital in Washington, Tyne and Wear on Monday April 23, was my first in 19 years as a professional.

I first realised I had a problem when I picked up a knock in training before the February trip to Charlton, my old club, and even though I had a scan I thought I could play on, and on. At first I thought the pain in my knee was just wear and tear, just normal aches and pains, but the pain became more frequent over the following six weeks or so. At first the knee would swell up after an hour but by the end it was swollen after about half that time.

I was missing more and more training sessions and at half-time in the game at Ipswich on April 14 I was forced to encase my knee in ice, while trying to keep it loose.

I have been lucky because I haven't had too many injuries which have restricted my career, but over the last season or so I have had more than ever before. Anyway, I did not expect to play against West Ham two days after the Ipswich defeat, but surprisingly I did not feel too bad on the Sunday. But after only half an hour my knee began to swell up – I played because we still needed a point to be mathematically safe – a poor situation to be in after a fine early part of the season when we were up near the top of the table and actually led it in early September after winning away at Coventry City.

Then Bobby asked me if I could make the derby clash with Sunderland on the following Saturday. I was desperate to play, especially as we needed revenge for their win at St James' early on in the season. But soon it became clear I would have no chance as I couldn't even train by the Thursday. So on the Friday before the game I was pulled out, and it was decided I would go into hospital for the operation on the following Monday.

Once again I watched the derby clash at home on television.

The operation was almost painless, it did not worry me at all, and straight away I was back in the gym looking forward to the day I could return and join in training with the lads. At least I am going to be fit for the start of the new season, my tenth at the club.

The time waiting to be able to kick a ball again was the longest period I had been out of the game in my whole career. Within days I was already missing the involvement and while I am not a good watcher, I will go to the home games and support the lads.

Once again people were left to ask me what my future held, as if this almost minor knee injury would stop me wanting to play for the Mags next season – no way. My aim is to play as many games as possible in 2001/02. The important things are that I believe I am still worth my place and that we improve our on previous performances.

I believe honestly that if we'd had all of our top players fit over the last ten months then we would have finished in the top six. Missing Alan Shearer, Carl Cort, Nicos Dabizas, Kieron Dyer and even myself at times, has cost us dear. The summer of 2001 will be a make-or-break time for this club and this team. I do not believe I am speaking out of turn, nor do I believe that my opinion is not supported by the manager. He knows we need three or four quality signings to make certain of that high placing.

The protracted discussions involving the EC and FIFA over the future of the current transfer system and transfer fees has caused more clubs than Newcastle United problems over the last few months. I can quite understand why the board of directors have maintained a tight hold on the purse strings. That is not to say Bobby has not been able to sign players, but it has meant we have not spent as heavily as we might like to have done. Some clubs, Leeds United being a prime example, ignored the whole uncertainty and spent heavily on players such as Rio Ferdinand and Robbie Keane – a little matter of £29 million to be exact.

The board at Newcastle have supported their managers fully over the last decade but now they must allow the current manager to spend wisely. I hope we have plenty to spend as we have had in the past, even though we have little to show for it, and certainly no silverware.

The stadium was expanded, rising high above the city skyline, its capacity a magnificent 52,000 and every second week the stadium was full to the rafters. And yet it takes a player with strong nerves to perform well under such expectation and pressure – mind you it is a wonderful, supportive pressure which most other clubs in the country would love.

So really it is quite ironic that when the support had been so massive, we had our worst home record since I arrived at the club. No-one is to blame but us, the players. We have no excuses except the fact that we have had so many important players out injured.

What of our two most famous stars, Alan Shearer and Kieron Dyer? Well, Kieron first. He is an amazing talent, a real star who can only get better. Let us hope he stays at the club to play for our supporters so he can reach the heights of his career with Newcastle United.

While he is being watched by so many other top clubs, and that does not surprise me at all, I have heard nothing from him to suggest he is on his way out of the Newcastle in the coming few months. His performances in 2000/01 were magnificent. He carried the hopes of our supporters on his shoulders at the tender age of 22. No club wants to lose its best players. We are no different and I know just how disappointed we all would be if he left. A fit Kieron Dyer is a great sight in a black-and-white shirt with 52,000 fans reacting to his every stride with the ball at his feet.

A fit Alan Shearer will still bring us 25 goals a season, no doubt. So to have him out for so much of the season really hurt us. His sheer presence would have caused some defences to fold or at least to allow other players in our team to benefit from their obsession with him. Do not forget, also, that we missed Carl Cort, another of our front-line strikers, for the majority of the campaign. But Carl, to his credit, came back with a great run of form at the end of the season when his goals record was superb. But how many times were they able to partner one another? The answer is a measly five occasions. Put them together and you have a pair which will bring 50 goals a season. Where would that have seen us in the table? Top six, I believe.

People were quick to knock Carl, but don't forget that before Bobby paid Wimbledon £7 million for him he had scored 15 goals from a wide role in a side which was relegated. He comes in, scores two goals in his first three appearances and then disaster strikes him – and he is out for months with a hamstring problem, the first major injury of his career. The he sustained ankle ligament damage in a post-season friendly at Exeter. Don't tell me it has not been a terrible season for us.

Carl's problem was that he wanted to be back too soon, he knew that people would be talking about him as a waste of money, but instead of rushing back he should have made sure he was over the injury. Mind you, at least he wanted to return to action as quickly as possible – not a bad trait to have! I am sure he will prove to be a great signing for the club, especially when Al is alongside him. Then let us see how our home form is.

One game which brought the club more bad publicity than any other was our ill-fated trip the to The Valley in February. It was a special match for me as the opening of the latest part of ground redevelopment made the Valley almost unrecognisable from when I last played there for the club. The welcome I received from their supporters was unbelievable – but then the match began and things gradually went wrong.

We did well for 20 minutes but then conceded two bad goals and the rest is history. Before the match I had trained a total of two or three days in the previous three weeks, and in the end I was substituted. Rightly so because I was rubbish!

In truth we fell away after a bright start, lost the match, flew out to La Manga and trained solidly for a week. Yet we received so much bad publicity for not returning home to Tyneside after the defeat by my former club that the real reason we went to Spain was quickly forgotten or intentionally swept under the carpet.

Understandably Bobby was upset with our overall performance, but it is not true that he spent the whole week in La Manga angry with us. He knew why we were there – to train on great pitches and give some of us the opportunity to train regularly away from terrible weather and muddy pitches back home. It was so bad at Chester Le Street that at times the lads had to train on astroturf covered in snow and ice.

However, we were shocked by the anger coming back in snippets from the press cuttings. I still believe it was a total over-reaction. We were made to feel as if we were having a holiday, which is absolutely stupid if you know the manager and the professionalism of the man. Does anyone think the chairman would have sent us away on a jaunt?

The manager's immediate after-match reaction was then multiplied many times over by other critics during the following days. Much of that appeared in the local press, which disappointed me more than anything else.

Bobby was so obviously disappointed because it was the first time we had been on national television for some time and to turn in such a poor show really upset him. But, I repeat, it did not take him long to get over it, although he had us training really hard every day. It was tough but we all came home feeling as if it had done us good, certainly those who needed it most.

Looking ahead to 2001/02, I was very much looking forward to my testimonial match. Have I really been here ten years? It seems only yesterday that Kevin Keegan told me Newcastle was closer to London than Middlesbrough!

My testimonial against Athletic Bilbao in August was an opportunity for everyone to come along and enjoy themselves, as in all of my time here there have been only two pre-season matches at St James' Park. Apart from that, it gave the fans a chance to see the players in a competitive game, having been starved of club football for the summer.

It is a privilege which I appreciated very much and I thank everyone for all of their help. Also I hope it helped the manager and his pre-season plans, with only days to go before the Premiership season commences.

As I look back on this book it is clear to me that every day is far from boring at Newcastle United. There is always something going on, always something which brings the club into the national spotlight. What do they say: any publicity is good publicity? I am not sure this is always the case, but life is never boring on Tyneside.

CHAPTER 14

JAMES IBISTER –
A DEDICATION

It would not have mattered if everything had gone wonderfully well for me on the pitch in 2000/2001, still it would have been a year I would remember for the loss of a friend. At the end of it I underwent my first football-related operation, to clear out some loose cartilage in my knee. And yet nothing as trivial as that really means much when I take into account the loss of one of my most supportive and wonderful fans.

While I worry about a little pain in my knee, there is a lovely family in Nottinghamshire who have lost their son. James Ibister died on January 9 after a brave battle against a rare disease called Marquios Syndrome, a malaise which, in layman's terms, is to do with enzyme deficiency, where the bones and cartilage do not grow. Children suffering this disease rarely live past their teens.

Only 50 children in the whole of the United Kingdom have come down with this rare complaint, but James, who I had known for seven years following a chance meeting in a Sheffield hotel, lost his battle at the unbelievably 'old' age of 21.

The news of his death, broken to me by his father Duncan during the early days of this new year, brought me down to earth with a bump. It was not just me, either. My family and the whole Newcastle United squad, including Bobby Robson, had got to know James and they were all equally stunned and upset.

During my darkest football days, when Ruud Gullit refused to give me the time of day, never mind a place in his team, James would be in touch telling me not to get too down. He was trying all the time to raise my spirits over the hardly life-threatening problems I faced in my career. All the while he was battling so bravely against his illness, and yet he never failed to think about others while refusing to talk about his own situation.

If football has given me anything it has given me much, much more because it allowed me to meet and then get to know James Ibister. That is more special than any medals or awards I might receive.

Yet, as I have already said, it was only a chance meeting which brought James, then aged 13, into my life – and would you believe it, his favourite player was not yours truly but the Magpies' centre-forward of the time who could not stop scoring goals, a certain Andy Cole!

It was 4 March 1994, a typical Friday evening on a typical away trip for Kevin Keegan's Newcastle United entertainers. We had booked into a Sheffield hotel when, as I walked through the lobby, I spotted this boy with a huge grin. He was in a wheelchair with his father in close attendance. While he did not have a replica strip on, it was clear he was a football fan, a Newcastle United fan. Soon I began to converse with James, who lived in Nuttall, and asked him why he didn't have a strip on. He told me, with a smile on his face, that his father would not buy him one.

I had a conversation with his father, who told me James had a long-term illness. I said I would send him a photograph. I said also that I would send him my shirt and then he wrote back telling me that Andy, who has since gone on to play for England as well as Manchester United, was his favourite Magpie. That day we had won 1–0 at Hillsborough with a last-minute winner from who else but Andy? It will stick in the memories of our supporters as we played in that one-off green strip, still a collectors' item among some of our fans. Anyway, I replied that maybe one day I might be his favourite Newcastle player.

From that moment on I got my wish and I became the player James followed so loyally. Gradually I built up a lovely friendship, not only with James but his family, too. Every time I got a shirt which meant something I would send it to James, including my 1998 World Cup shirt and my Newcastle FA Cup Final shirt, and they were all placed lovingly on his wall. However, he gave me back more than I could ever give him.

I will never forget his face, always smiling whenever I saw him; it is something I will always remember about him. We just clicked and would talk about so many different subjects. Nothing will ever dim my recollection of those conversations, which took place over several years and always featured his favourite subjects. Dr Who was a mutual interest, he knew every actor who had played the role, but his choice of music left a little more to be desired. He liked Bon Jovi, Sinead O'Connor and Alice Cooper – none were to my own taste, but who cared?

James will always live on in my memory. I'm not being sentimental, that's simply a fact!

I will never forget his funeral in Nuttall, which I felt honoured to attend along with my wife Anna. It was the first time we met Duncan's wife Kristine. She explained how they had had adopted James when he was seven. Clearly they had given him an enormous amount of love during his cruelly short life.

That day his favourite Alice Cooper and Bon Jovi music was played. His preferred song was Alice Cooper's very early anthem, School's Out.

He will never be forgotten by anyone who came into contact with him. I remember the last time I saw him, it was before the game at Derby County on December 23. We lost 2–0 and I got injured. Anyway, the rest of the lads took time out to meet and talk with James, they made a right fuss over him – which his family really appreciated – before I introduced him to Bobby Robson. The gaffer was great, as you would expect. He spent 20 minutes or so talking with James and made the young man's day.

When I saw him that day he was almost lying down in his chair and I remember that he looked so well. So you can guess how devastated I was when his father rang me only a couple of weeks later to tell me of James' death. I could not believe it, it was a sad, sad day. When I told everyone they were lost for words and Bobby was genuinely upset.

It shows just how important it is to take time out to appreciate your fans. That is something which we can give back to people and footballers should never, ever, relinquish that duty to respect every single supporter. They give us so much and my friend James Ibister, in particular, gave me so much. He had all those problems and yet sent me letters and would ring me to show his support when I was not being picked by Gullit.

When I have my testimonial match in August, I will have James' family up for the occasion. The sad thing is that James himself will not be there.

So do not expect me to worry too much over my knee operation, because there is always someone else much worse off, even if they tend to care more about others than worry about their own problems. My friendship with that remarkable young man put everything else into perspective. People worry about the silliest of things. None of it really matters. Family and health are all that really matter.

This is why I dedicate this book
to James Ibister.

CAREER STATISTICS

CHARLTON ATHLETIC

Season	League app/goals	FA Cup app/goals	League Cup app/goals	Members' Cup app/goals	Anglo-Italian Cup/Play offs app/goals	Total app/goals
1983/84	10(1)/4	-/-	-/-	-/-	-/-	10(1)/4
1984/85	36(3)/10	2/0	2/0	-/-	-/-	40(3)/10
1985/86	26(9)/8	1/0	1(1)/0	0(1)/0	-/-	28(11)/8
1986/87	29(4)/3	-/-	3/1	4(1)/3	2/0 (PO)	38(5)/7
1987/88	22(1)/2	1/0	2(1)/0	1/0	-/-	26(2)/2
1988/89	25(6)/5	3/1	0(1)/0	1/0	-/-	29(7)/6
1989/90	37/1	3/1	3/0	1/0	-/-	44/2
1990/91	43/13	1/0	2/0	-/-	-/-	46/13
1991/92	39/12	3/0	3/0	-/-	-/-	45/12
1992/93	7/1	-/-	-/-	-/-	1/0 (AIC)	8/1
TOTAL	274(24)/59	14/2	16(3)/1	7(2)/3	3/0	314(29)/65

At the end of the 1999/2000 season, Robert Lee was 17th in Charlton's all-time appearance table and 15th in the all-time goal table.

NEWCASTLE UNITED

Season	League app/goals	FA Cup app/goals	League Cup app/goals	Europe app/goals	Total app/goals
1992/93	36/10	4/2	3/1	-/-	43/13
1993/94	41/7	3/0	3/1	-/-	47/8
1994/95	35/9	4/1	2/0	3/4	44/14
1995/96	38/8	1/0	4/1	-/-	41/9
1996/97	33/5	2/1	1/0	8/0	44/6
1997/98	28/4	6/0	2/0	6/0	42/4
1998/99	26/0	3/0	-/-	1/0	30/0
1999/2000	29/0	4/1	1/0	6/0	40/1
2000/01	22/0	3/0	1/0	0/0	26/0
TOTAL	288/43	30/5	17/3	24/4	357/56

ENGLAND

21 caps, scoring 2 goals:
v Romania at Wembley in a 1-1 draw, 12 October 1994
v South Africa at Old Trafford in a 2-1 win, 24 May 1997

INDEX